To
Che, Robin, Rebecca and Tom

An illustration of the work involved in the fork grinding process of the Sheffield cutlery trade. Considered medical opinion of the day stated that dry fork grinding was the most destructive of all the grinding trades carried on at Sheffield, many of the workers being 'cut off' before the age of 30. As seen here, the trade was carried on in a building called a 'wheel'. There were said to be 96 'wheels' in and around Sheffield, 80 being steam-powered and 16 being powered by water. The room in which the work was performed was known as a 'hull'. Boys began light work from ages of 9 to 13; heavier tasks commenced with the 12-14 year old groups.

A Vfe

Child Labour Through the Nineteenth Century

Alan Bennett

Published by
Waterfront Publications
463 Ashley Road, Parkstone, Poole, Dorset BH14 0AX

© Alan Bennett and Waterfront Publications
ISBN 0 946184 66 6   1991

Typeset by PageMerger, Southampton, Hampshire
Printed by The Alden Press, Oxford

Contents

Boys under instruction in tailoring at the South Metropolitan District school, Sutton, 1872. The District schools, schools of industry and the Ragged Schools all served similar purpose in as far as they concerned themselves with the condition of pauper children and those generally without means. Education and training were combined, the district schools, for example, taking children from several Unions (workhouses) to train them in habits of gainful employment and respectability. Edward Tufnell, Assistant Poor Law Commissioner, wrote: "I am aware that it is costly, but it is cheaper than allowing them to become thieves, paupers or prostitutes as was the case, formerly." London, Manchester, Liverpool and Leeds had the first records for such initiatives.

Introduction

This book has been written to tell something of the story of children at work during the last century. There were as many stories as there were children, for the most part, their actual experiences, far removed from today's popular conception, are not widely known in any detail. Actual conditions depended upon all manner of circumstances as, hopefully, the book will reveal, but the main focus here is to identify the particular individual and his or her experience, within the nineteenth century social and economic context.

All the material is presented around a number of specific industries and occupations, and is confined largely to the period 1830-1880. It begins with the early Factory Reform Movement and ends, in almost every case, with the introduction of compulsory elementary education, itself linking with related developments in employment legislation.

Wherever available, the actual contemporary evidence has been used, the purpose being to develop the narrative/documentary approach, allowing the people of the book to come across as directly, and in as immediate a manner as possible. The intention is to illustrate the circumstances and influences that actually defined and shaped working-class lives.

The theme of children at work is one to which people, past and present, have responded, for all manner of reasons. Child labour offers a study which goes far beyond descriptions of the all too frequent physical exploitation. It is a study which encompasses broad outline themes—society's attitudes generally to children, to working people overall, to a climate of opinion and response, basic values as to work, personal responsibility etc.. It is also a study of numerous related factors; questions of employer's expectations and role, of parental attitudes, examples of housing and general health, as defined by the growing public health movement; of obvious economic pressures and a society functioning under the principles of the Poor Law, together with questions on the role of government itself. The vitally important issue centring on the conflicting/competing claims of employment as against educational opportunity (even necessity) must also be recognised. This, of course, underlines the serious moral dimensions involved.

Whatever one's approach to the subject of child labour, comparisons and contrasts are inevitable; on the one hand, between nineteenth-century society and the values and experience of our own day, and, on the other, between the many different shades of opinion that characterized the debate within the nineteenth-century itself. There were detailed differences within particular industries: e.g; mining and agriculture, depending upon local or regional conditions; even those concerned to implement reform frequently came into dispute over questions of motive, means and ends. Irony and paradox was apparent across the entire question of child labour. Developments in our own day share similarities.

Regardless of one's motives for studying the past, the issue of child labour rarely fails to challenge our emotions or our perspectives. Numerous comparisons are readily drawn today between the past record of, say, South Lancashire, Mid Lothian, Somerset or East Anglia, and that of present-day experience in Kanchipuran, Uttar Pradesh, Thailand or the Phillipines. The subject is thus given its international context across time and place, but it is the process of time, not their actual circumstances, that separate Third World children today from their forerunners described in this book. Even though Western society has witnessed extensive social reform since the last century, there is, today, no room for complacency. This would be to ignore or reject the example of history. Whilst we might well be better informed as to present conditions in the Third World than, perhaps, many Victorians were (or wished to be) about their own society, are we necessarily any more actively concerned about the countless children under exploitation today?

Alan Bennett
October 1990

4

Chapter One
Factory Reform

In 1771 Richard Arkwright opened a cotton mill at Cromford in Derbyshire. He had developed a shinning machine known as the Water Frame which was to mark the beginning of a new era for the cotton trade in terms of production and organisation. Arkwright's Water Frame was powered by water from the River Derwent and was too large to be usefully employed in any traditional household or workshop. The new machinery needed its own purpose-built premises together with a large organised workforce, and so marked the beginnings of the Factory Age and its large scale production focused on the mill, and regulated through a specific code of conduct. Arkwright went on to open more mills in Derbyshire, Nottingham and Manchester, for example, eventually receiving a knighthood for his efforts.

The Spinning Mule of 1779, invented by Samuel Crompton, made it possible to produce a strong but fine thread and became the standard spinning machine of the Factory Age. This, and the gradual application of steam power to the mills through James Watt's development of rotary motion, (1785) represented two further milestones in progress. These and various other improvements, together with the concentration of the cotton industry on the South Lancashire coalfield, gave rise to the great manufacturing towns of which Manchester (Cottonopolis) was the commercial capital, and, Liverpool the great cotton port.

The cotton trade became the first of Britain's manufacturing industries to become factory based and its valuable role in the economy gave it a tremendous importance in terms of overall industrial growth. By the early years of the nineteenth century cotton production was to a very large extent mechanised with child labour playing a decisive role in its success.

The Factory Reform Movement

Of all the many forms of employment followed by children and young people in the nineteenth century the

A view of cotton workers from the early 1860s, the period of the cotton famine. This great Lancashire industry suffered extensively from the effects of the American Civil War, when the vital raw material from the Southern States was not to be had. Set against the backdrop of the mills, a cross-section of the workforce is seen here. Without regular employment, the working people were inevitably subject to considerable hardship, being left to the devices of the poor law. Those in more fortunate circumstances were helped by benevolent mill owners, providing them with basic essentials.

Two illustrations of work in a cotton mill as presented in 'The History of Cotton Manufacture', Edward Baines, 1836. Baines took the view that, overall, this employment was not harmful to children, and that it could well be beneficial. The first view shows women and young girls at work in the carding, drawing and roving room of Messrs. Swainson, Burley and Company near Preston. In this preparatory work for spinning, the cotton is straightened, laid parallel and run together to give consistency and strength, the thread being further drawn out and twisted. The second view shows young people mule spinning. They are able to operate large machines without any great difficulty, thereby making it an ideal labour force; competent, generally docile and cheap to employ. Note also the scavenger, the boy cleaning beneath the machine whilst it is at work. Both illustrations present a somewhat idealised view of factory life, stressing order, cleanliness and an overall positive appearance on the part of the workers themselves in their stature and dress.

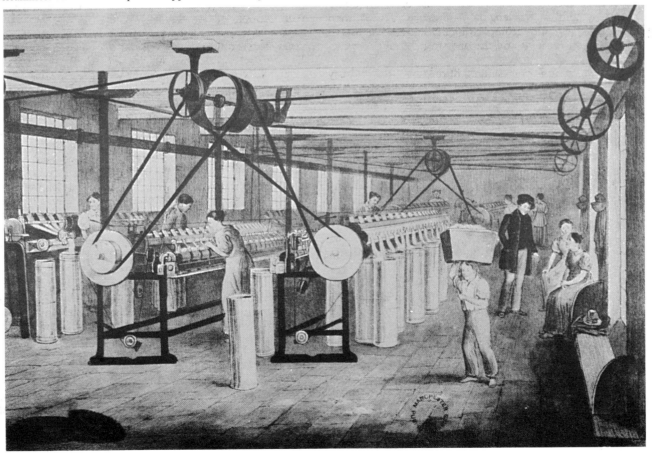

circumstances of those at work within the textile mills are probably the best known.

The Report of the Select Committee on Factory Children's Labour (1831-32), makes for compelling, if somewhat disturbing reading, illustrating the situation of children set to work at the machines. Hard, physical work involving long hours was nothing new for children, as agriculture and domestic industry had traditionally employed large numbers of children and young people. The decisive difference between factory work and more traditional pursuits was nevertheless clear. Factory employment imposed a strict discipline and order which was expected to be obeyed without question. Confined within the factory, often behind locked doors, the pace of work was dictated by the machine; initially water power, and eventually steam.

Strict timekeeping and the subjection to tireless machinery served to destroy any sense of independence as, indeed, did the numerous fines relating to every aspect of behaviour. Financial penalties were imposed for all manner of offences, ranging from the waste or spoiling of materials, opening windows, or leaving their allocated work place whistling, to failing to find a replacement worker in the event of illness. For the skilled hand-loom weaver in particular the impact of mechanisation was extremely drastic, removing, as it did, their status in the working community and reducing them to the situation of machine minder.

Given the nature of factory work, which for the most part involved tending the machinery, it was considered employment well suited to children, with the added attraction that their labour came cheap. Children worked in large numbers as 'piecers' – joining broken threads on the spinning machines, 'doffers' – those who removed full or loaded bobbins, replacing them with empty ones on the spinning machines, and as 'scavengers' – those who performed cleaning duties. The accompanying tables show full lists of employment, earnings and the age range of all those employed.

The working day for children during the 'brisk' or busy time could keep them at the machines for up to sixteen to eighteen hours in conditions made intolerable for many by strict discipline enforced by physical punishment. Many examples are recorded of children receiving beatings, strappings or other similar punishments for errors in their work, for misbehaviour, or, indeed, for the purpose of keeping them awake and alert towards the end of a long day.

Accidents were also common, given the absence of any safety regulations, and were largely inevitable as children were hurried or fatigued. Parental influence was not easy to exercise as many parents had little choice but witness ill-treatment towards theirs or other children by the overseer. Parents, like their children, were invariably in desperate need of the collective family wage, and were therefore in no position to protest effectively. Pauper apprentices, lacking even the support of parents, were the property of the mill and were entirely dependent upon the goodwill of their employer.

It was to the pauper apprentices that Parliament first addressed itself, passing an Act in 1802 to preserve the health and morals of these children in the cotton and woollen mills. Under the Act, apprentices were not to be employed for more than 12 hours a day. Provision was also included for their education:

That every such apprentice shall be instructed, in some part of every working day, for the first four years at least of his or hers apprenticeship, in the usual hours of work in reading, writing and arithmetic or either of them according to the age and ability of such apprentice, by some discreet and proper person to be provided and paid by the master or mistress of such apprentice in some room or place in such mill or factory to be set apart for that purpose.

A further Act of 1819, introduced by Robert Peel, attempted to prevent the employment of all children under nine years of age. It also limited children over the age of nine to a 12 hour day. The two Acts achieved very little, however, as in both cases there was no real provision for inspection and enforcement except that exercised by the Justice of the Peace.

The cotton spinners of Warrington wrote to Robert Peel on 27 March 1818 in the hope that they might contribute to the success of the forthcoming Factory Bill. Their letter included the following description of working life.

The principal cotton mills here work from half-past five in the morning till half-past eight at night, so that the poor children are called out of bed at five, and it is nine at night when they get home, some of them being under six, many under eight years of age. We feel exquisitely for these in the winter time, coming out of the warm bed, clothed in rags or half naked, through the frost, cold, snow winds and rain, many of them barefoot, into the hot room where no air is permitted to enter that can be prevented, as it is injurious in the spinning of cotton.

In giving further detail the spinners related how their employer had threatened dismissal to anyone found signing their petition, adding that he had taken advantage of the distressed force of 27 persons, aged from six to twenty-one years, who received collectively only 27 shillings per week. During slack periods the mill was closed for up to a fortnight, whilst in the brisk time they were compelled to work up to fifteen hours a day.

One of the best known and thorough denunciations of factory conditions came in the famous article 'Yorkshire Slavery' written by Richard Oastler and published in the Leeds Mercury on 16 October 1830. The following is an extract from this powerful and emotionally charged work.

Let truth speak out, appalling as the statement may appear. The fact is true. Thousands of our fellow-creatures and fellow-subjects, both male and female, the miserable inhabitants of a Yorkshire town (Yorkshire now represented in Parliament by the giant of anti-slavery principles) are this very moment existing in a state of slavery, more horrid than are the victims of that hellish system 'colonial slavery'. These innocent creatures drawl out, unpitied, their short but miserable existence, in a place famed for its profession of religious zeal, whose inhabitants are ever foremost in professing 'temperance' and 'reformation', and are striving to outrun their neighbours in missionary exertion, and would fain send the Bible to the farthest corner of the globe – aye, in the very place where the anti-slavery fever rages most furiously, her apparent charity is not admired on earth, than her real cruelty is abhorred in Heaven. The very streets which receive droppings of

Cotton workers waiting for their breakfast, stand in Mr Chapman's courtyard at Mottram, near Manchester. Chapman was one such concerned employer, anxious to see the workforce provided for.

an 'Anti Slavery Society' are every morning wet by the tears of innocent victims at the accursed shrine of avarice, who are compelled (not by the cart-whip of the negro slave-driver) but by the dread of the equally appalling thong or strap of the over-looker, to hasten, half-dressed, but not half-fed, to those magazines of British infantile slavery – the worsted mills in the town and neighbourhood of Bradford!!!

Thousand of little children, both male and female, but principally female, from seven to fourteen years of age, are daily compelled to labour from six o'clock in the morning to seven in the evening, with only – Britons, blush while you read it! – with only thirty minutes allowed for eating and recreation. Poor infants! ye are indeed sacrificed at the shrine of avarice, without even the solace of the negro slave; ye are no more than he is, free agents; ye are compelled to work as long as the necessity of your needy parents may require, or the cold-blooded avarice of your worse than barbarians masters may demand! Ye live in the boasted land of freedom, and feel and mourn that ye are slaves, and slaves without the only comfort which the negro has. He knows it is his sordid, mercenary master's interest that he should live, be strong and healthy. No so wish you. Ye are doomed to labour from morning to night for one who cares not how soon your weak and tender frames are stretched to breaking. You are not mercifully valued at so much per head; this would assure you at least (even with the worst and most cruel masters) of the mercy shown to their labouring beasts. No, no! your soft and delicate limbs are tired and fagged, and jaded, at only so much per week, and when your

joints can act no longer, your emaciated frames are instantly supplied with other victims, who in this boasted land of liberty are HIRED – not sold – as slaves and daily forced to hear that they are free.

In an obviously contrasting, yet telling style, a similar story emerged through the evidence collected from the workforce in the Report of the Select Committee of Factory Children's Labour 1831-32. Here is the evidence of Samuel Coulson (describing working conditions for his daughters) and that of Charles Burns, a young employee in a flax mill at Leeds:

WHERE do you live? – Stanningley.

Where is that? – Near Leeds.

What is your trade? – A tailor.

Have you a family? – Yes.

Have any of them worked in a mill? – Yes, three daughters.

At what age did they begin to work? – The elder was going 12, and the middlemost going 11, and the youngest only 8 when they went to the mill first; they are older now.

At what time in the morning, in the brisk time, did those girls go to the mills? – In the brisk time, for about six weeks, they have gone at 3 o'clock in the morning, and ended at 10, or nearly half past, at night.

What sort of mills were those? – The worsted mills.

What intervals were allowed for rest or refreshment during those nineteen hours of labour? – Breakfast a quarter of an hour, and dinner half an hour and drinking time a quarter of an hour.

Is that all? – Yes.

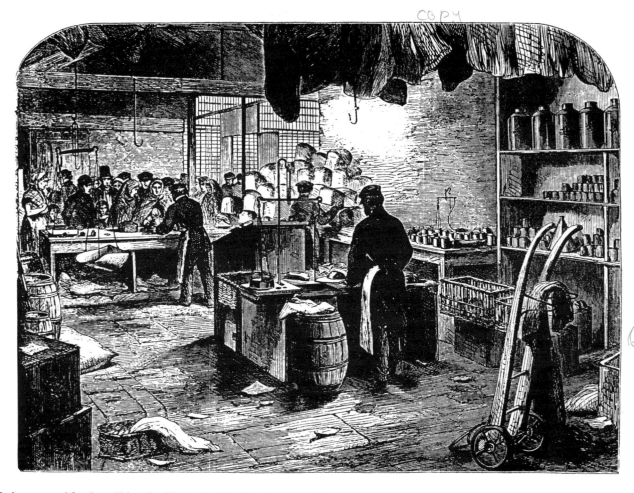

A shop opened for the mill-hands of Burley's Mill, Manchester are shown in November 1862. Mr Burley maintained an entire workforce of 1000 on support of between two and five shillings a week. Provisions included tea, coffee, soup, beans, bacon, rice pepper, flour etc., with, it was said, some 30 sacks of flour and ½ ton of bacon being used each week. Coal was also made available, being supplied from the Castle Field Coal Wharf. The Illustrated London News stated that Burley's activities represented "a noble example of what a right-minded man with ample means may do in such a crisis as the present."

Was any of that time taken up in cleaning the machinery? – They generally had to do what they call dry down; sometimes this took the whole of the time at breakfast or drinking, and they were to get their dinner or breakfast as they could; if not, it was brought home. Sometimes they could not get their breakfast at all? – Sometimes they could not.

How long ago was this? – It is better than a year since.

Had you not great difficulty in awakening your children to this excessive labour? – Yes, in the early time we had them to take up asleep and shake them, when we got them on the floor to dress them, before we could get them off to their work; but not so in the common hours.

What were the common hours? – Six o'clock at morning till half-past 8 at night.

Supposing they had been a little too late, what would have been the consequence during the long hours? – They were quartered in the longest hours, the same as in the shortest time.

What do you mean by quartering? – A quarter was taken off.

If they had been how much too late? – Five minutes.

What was the length of time they could be in bed during those long hours? – It was near 11 o'clock before we could get them into bed after getting a little victuals, and then at morning my mistress used to stop up all night, for fear that we could not get them ready for the time; sometimes we have gone to bed, and one of us generally woke.

What time did you get them up in the morning? – In general me or my mistress got up at 2 o'clock to dress them.

So that they had not above four hours sleep at this time? – No, they had not.

For how long together was it? – About six weeks it held; it was only done when the throng was very much on; it was not often that.

the common hours of labour were from 6 in the morning till half-past 8 at night? – Yes.

With the same intervals for food? – Yes, just the same.

Were the children excessively fatigued by this labour? – Many times; we have cried often when we have given them the little victualling we had to give them; we had

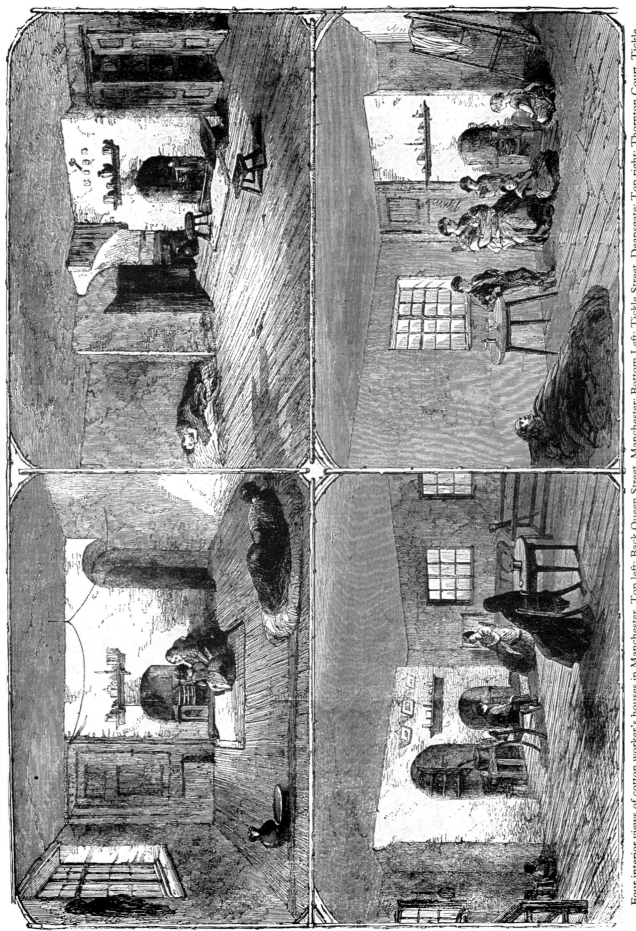

Four interior views of cotton worker's houses in Manchester. Top left: Back Queen Street, Manchester; Bottom Left; Tickle Street, Deansgate; Top right: Thornton Court, Tickle Street; Bottom right; Southern Street, Liverpool Road. Circumstances obviously varied even here. Note the attempt at some simple level of domesticity with the picture, shelves and basic furniture, notably at Tickle Street, lower left, where the household was clearly not confined to one room. The other views compare less favourably, with little evidence of the ability to provide. Note the rough bedding on the floor – even here the conditions were far more favourable than those of cellar dwellings. The lack of sanitation, adequate water, the ever-present damp and poor ventilation are suggested here but cannot easily be portrayed.

An illustration of cellar dwellings in London crammed with young children and women seeking the only shelter available to them. Such places, lacking any positive amenities other than the crudest shelter, were breeding grounds of disease and hopelessness amongst their inhabitants. Illustrations from the mid 1850s.

to shake them, and they have fallen to sleep with the victuals in their mouths many a time.

Had any of them any accident in consequence of this labour? – Yes, my eldest daughter when she went first there; she had been about five weeks, and used to fettle the frames when they were running, and my eldest girl agreed with one of the others to fettle hers that time, that she would do her work; while she was learning more about the work, the overlooker came by and said, "Ann, what are you doing there?" she said, "I am doing it for my companion, in order that I may know more about it;" he said, "Let go, drop it this minute," and the cog caught her fore-finger nail, and screwed it off below the knuckle, and she was five weeks in Leeds Infirmary

Has she lost that finger? – It is cut off at the second joint.

Were her wages paid during that time? – As soon as the accident happened the wages were totally stopped, indeed, I did not know which way to get her cured, and I do not know how it would have been cured but for the Infirmary.

Were the wages stopped at the half-day? – She was stopped a quarter of a day; it was done about four o'clock.

She had no sort of assistance from her employer during that time? – No.

You had no present made on that occasion? – No, not a farthing from any one.

Did this excessive term of labour occasion much cruelty also? – Yes, with being so much fatigued the strap was very frequently used.

Have any of your children been strapped? – Yes, every one; the eldest daughter; I was up in Lancashire a fortnight, and when I got home I saw her shoulders, and I said, "Ann, what is the matter?" she said, "The overlooker has strapped me;" but, she said, "do not go to the overlooker, for if you do we shall lose our work;" I said I would not if she would tell me the truth as to what caused it. "Well," she said, "I will tell you, father." She says, "I was fettling the waste, and the girl I had learning had got so perfect she could keep the side up till I could fettle the waste; the overlooker came round, and said, "What are you doing?" I said, "I am fettling, while the other girl keeps the upper end up;" he said, "Drop it this minute;" she said, "No, I must go on with this;" and because she did not do it, he took the strap, and beat her between the shoulders. My wife was out at the time, and when she came in she said her back was beat nearly to a jelly; and the rest of the girls encouraged her to go to Mrs. Varley, and she went to he, and she rubbed it with a part of a glass of rum, and gave her an old silk handkerchief to cover the place till it got well.

Did you observe those marks a fortnight after? – Yes. So that she had to be dressed in her wounds something in a way of a poor soldier that has suffered at the halberts? – We could not get the rum to dress it with, but we got some milk and water; and she told me that she bathed it with it till it was completely well.

You could not afford any medical person to visit your daughter when so cruelly used? – No; all I could get to take her to the Infirmary in Leeds was 2d., and I laid 1d. of it for an orange; I thought she would fall sick, and I bought one penny roll with the other; and that was all I got between Stanningley and Leeds, and Leeds and Stanningley again.

You are a man in indigent circumstances? – Yes.

But a kind and indulgent parent? – I will do anything for my children that are honest.

Was the overlooker that used your child so discharged? – Not at that time, but he was afterwards, about ten weeks afterwards, but not on that account; after she lost her finger, it was ordered that they should not fettle while the machinery was running.

What was the wages in the short hours? – Three shillings a week each.

When they wrought those very long hours what did they get? – Three shillings and seven-pence halfpenny. For all that additional labour they had only 7½d. a week additional? – No more. Could you dispose of their wages, when they had received them as you wished: did you understand that? – They never said any thing to me, but the children have said, "If we do not bring some little from the shop I am afraid we shall lose our work;" and sometimes they used to bring a bit of sugar or some little oddment, generally of their own head.

That is, they were expected to lay out part of their wages under the truck system? – Yes.

What were the articles in which they dealt? – Meal and flour, and all the other vegetables, and such like, and wearing apparel.

Had your children any opportunity of sitting during those long days of labour? – No; they were in general, whether there was work for them to do or not, to move backwards and forwards till something came to their hands.

Do you know any of the mills where seats are provided for children where they may rest, when not immediately employed? – Yes, only one concern, at Mr. Wood's of Bradford.

Has he provided seats? – Yes, as this may be the frame the seats are lodged

COMMITTEE ON FACTORIES BILL
Charles Burns, called in and Examined
Where do your live? – No. 26, Duke Street, Leeds.
What age are you? – Going on 14.
Have you worked at mills? – Yes.
At what age did you begin work in them? – I was nearly 8 years old.
In whose mill did you first work? – Marshall's.
Was that a flax mill? – Yes.
In what department of that mill did you work? – I was a bobbin-doffer.
How many hours a day did you work? – From 6 in the morning till 7 at night.
What time had you allowed for your meals? – Forty minutes at dinner.

Had you any time allowed you for breakfast or drinking? – No.

Did that labour fatigue you very much? – Yes.

You found yourself very much tired? – Yes, as soon as I went home and sat down by the fire, I fell asleep directly.

Where did you go to work after you left that place? – At Mr. Leighton's, in Lancashire.

Was it at the same sort of mill? – Yes; we worked there from 6 to half-past 7, and sometimes 8 o'clock.

What were the times allowed you there for your meals? – A quarter of an hour at breakfast, forty minutes at dinner, and ten minutes at drinking.

Did you find that very fatiguing work to you? – Yes.

Where did you remove to then? – To Mr. Hive's, of Leeds.

What were your hours of working there? – From half-past 5 in the morning till 8 at night.

Had you any time allowed for breakfast there? – No. Nor for your drinking? – No.

How much time had you allowed for your dinner? – Forty minutes.

Had you sometimes to clean the machinery at your dinner hour? – Yes, and had to wipe all the machines.

How long did that take you generally? – About a quarter of an hour, and sometime 20 minutes.

Pray how often were you allowed to make water? – Three times a day.

And were you allowed to make water at any time that you wanted? – No; only when a boy came to tell you that it was your turn, and whether we wanted or no, that was the only time allowed us; if we did not go when he came round, we could not go at all.

Did he go to you in succession, to one part of the mill first, and so round the whole? – Yes; he started at one end as soon as ever he came to the mill, and then went all round.

Did those who were nearer to the entrance have to go out directly? – He starts at one end, goes down one side, and then down another, then up again.

Would they let you go out, if you asked, at a different time? – No, we could not go, however much we wanted.

Could you hold your water all that time? – No; we were forced to let it go.

In fact, you yourself could not retain your urine long? – No.

Did you the spoil or wet your clothes constantly? – Every noon, and every night.

Did you ever hear of that hurting anybody? – Yes, there was a boy died.

Did he go home ill with attempting to suppress his urine? – Yes; and after he had been home a bit, he died.

Were you beaten at your work? – If we looked off our work, or spoke to one another, we were beaten.

If you had not gone so fast as the machine, should you have been beaten? – If we let the machine stop half a minute we should have been beaten.

What did they call that sort of work you did? – Screwing.

Was that rather hard employment? – Yes; and we were kept at that from morning to night.

When you retired for the purposes of nature, how long would they allow you to stop? – If we were longer than five minutes we got beat; and if we stopped longer they would not let us go out another time when it was our turn.

What time of the day was it you were most beaten? – In the morning.

And when you were sleepy? – Yes.

What were you beat for? – If we looked off our work, or looked at one another, or spoke.

Was the mill very dusty? – Yes.

What effect had it upon your health? – I had very bad health.

Why? – The dust got down my throat.

What effect did it produce? – When we went home at night and went to bed, we spit up blood.

Is the flax mill so dusty in some parts that you can hardly see one another? – Yes.

Is it not likewise, in what is called hot-water spinning, extremely hot in these mills? – Yes, very hot.

Is not the place full of steam? – Yes, and the machinery throws off water perpetually; so that we are wet to the skin by the hot water.

Then your clothes are entirely wet? – Yes; and as soon as we get home our clothes are quite stiff with the frost in the winter-time.

Had you a cough with inhaling that dust? – Yes; I had a cough; and spit blood.

What did you get for your breakfast and drinking? – I had tea, sometimes coffee, and butter and bread; and my tea, for fear of wanting to make water, I used to throw out of the window.

Did any other boys do that too? – Yes, many did, because of the dust.

And did many others throw their tea out of the window for the same reason as you did? – Yes.

In either of those mills, Mr. Marshall's or Mr. Hive's, were you allowed to sit down? – No.

Were you not allowed to sit down during the whole of the day? – If we did we should get beaten; we had nothing to sit on unless we sat upon the frame by getting upon it.

Is it a common thing for you children to be beaten in this sort of way? – Yes, there used to be screaming among the boys and girls every time of the day, and they made black and blue marks on their shoulders.

Then there was a continual beating either of one child or another going on? – Yes.

Where was this? – At Mr. Hive's.

Was there a beating going on at Mr. Marshall's? – They did not beat them so much as at Mr. Hive's.

Where did you go to then? – To Mr. Moses Atkinson's.

Is that a flax mill? – Yes.

What length of time did you work there when trade was brisk? – From 6 in the morning till half-past 7 and sometimes 8, and when in full work from half-past 5 till half-past 7.

Did they beat you up to the work there also? – Yes.

State whether it is the general system at those mills to beat the doffers?

Always; those that are last get seven stripes over the hand; one is sure to be last.

What do the doffers do? – Take the full bobbins off, and put on the empty ones.

Those are the least, then, are the worst beaten? – No, sometimes the least are last, and sometimes the largest. Just as it happens? – Yes.

Has there been a great deal of beating? – Yes.

And the same system of cruelty is persevered in? – Yes.

Are you most beaten at the end of the day? – If you let the machines stand when they have got anything on them, you are beaten.

Are accidents often occurring at these mills? – Yes.

State any that occurred within your own knowledge? – I had a sister who worked at Marshall's, and she got killed there by accident.

Did the overlooker behave ill to the children when your sister was working there? – Yes, he behaved very bad.

Did he beat your sister? – Yes.

Did he beat the rest of the children also? – Yes.

Since there has been talk of the Ten Hours' Bill, do they allow a little time to get breakfast in? – Yes, a quarter of an hour to breakfast and ten minutes to drinking.

The poor man's friend. This famous cartoon from 'Punch' requires little explanation. Note the workhouse seen through the broken window, another prominent feature in the lives of the poor. Death was also a frequent and inevitable visitor amongst the very young. Infant mortality, for example, in working areas ran remarkably high, the death of young children being a commonplace of nineteenth century society. In the period circa 1840, 57% of children in working areas (Manchester), died before the age of five.

The shop, referred to in the first extract, was that operated by the factory. Workers were often expected, under threat of dismissal, to spend a proportion of their wage at these shops where they could expect to buy inferior goods at inflated prices. The truck system, as it was known, was strongly opposed by the more enlightened factory owners such as Robert Owen and John Fielden, but it was widespread across many branches of industry in the first half of the nineteenth century. (See also chapters on the coal mines and lace industry)

Together with the discipline and long hours children and adults had also to endure an unhealthy working environment. In evidence to the commissioners for both cotton and woollen mills, young people described the effects of intense heat, with temperatures at or above 80 degrees. They also told of the great contrasts there could be within different parts of the factories and of the considerable difference in temperature on leaving work to return home, especially in winter. Constant exposure to cotton dust and steam in the air had an effect upon the lungs, with all these conditions contributing to such diseases as pneumonia and consumption. With these circumstances then allied to long hours it was scarcely surprising that many workers became physically deformed, standing or leaning across the machinery on seemingly endless shifts.

Edward Baines, in his "History of the Cotton Manufacture in Great Britain" 1835 offered a different view. He wrote: "The labour is light and requires very little muscular exertion. Attention and gentle exercise are needed .... it is scarcely possible for any employment to be lighter. The children's manner .. is more frequently sportive than gloomy."

Having drawn attention to what we would see as the harsh environment of the factory, it is important also to acknowledge a very significant point from the Report on the 'Sanitary Conditions of the Labouring Population, 1842'. Credited to Edwin Chadwick overall, the report offers an interesting insight into comparative conditions between the factory and the children's own homes.

It was pointed out that, in Manchester, amongst the labouring population, 57 per cent of children died before 5 years of age. Furthermore, it was reported that, in certain respects, life could be more healthy in the mills than at home. This was certainly true of many of the working people's homes:

'However defective the ventilation of many of the factories may yet be, they are all of them dryer and more equally warm than the residence of the parent, and we had proof that weakly children have been put into better-managed factories as healthier places for them than their own homes.'

The Report also showed that both Liverpool, and London's Bethnal Green, the former a port and commercial community, the latter, a centre of domestic style production within the home, had worse death rates overall than Manchester, an industrial manufacturing centre. The condition of Liverpool was particularly bad.

Another notorious slum, the King's Arms yard, coal-yard, Drury Lane.

Middle class homes were reported to have had a higher death rate amongst the 5 to 10 year age group in Manchester than those of the working class. This was a point made by those in favour of using children's labour in the factories and does throw an interesting light upon living conditions – the Public Health debate overall.

Dr. Baron Howard described conditions in the poor districts of Manchester in 1840. His work also contributed to Chadwick's Sanitary Report of 1842:

'That the filthy and disgraceful state of many of the streets in these densely populated and neglected parts of the town where the indigent poor chiefly reside cannot fail to exercise a most baneful influence over their health is an inference which experience has fully proved to be well founded; and no fact is better established than that a large proportion of the causes of fever which occur in Manchester originate in these situations. Of the 182 patients admitted into the temporary fever hospital in Balloon Street, 135 at least came from unpaved or otherwise filthy streets, or from confined and dirty courts and alleys. Many of the streets in which cases of fever are common are so deep in mire, or so full of hollows and heaps of refuse that the vehicle used for conveying the patients to the House of Recovery often cannot be driven along them and the patients are obliged to be carried to it from considerable distances. Whole streets in these quarters are unpaved and without drains or main sewers, are worn into deep ruts and holes, in which water constantly stagnates, and are so covered with refuse and excrementitious matter as to be almost impassable from depth of mud, and intolerable from stench.

In the narrow lanes, confined courts and alleys, leading from these, similar nuisances exist, if possible, to a still greater extent; and as ventilation is here more obstructed, their effects are still more pernicious. In many of these places are to be seen privies in the most disgusting state of filth, open cesspools, obstructed drains, ditches full of stagnant water, dunghills, pigsties, etc., from which the most abominable odours are emitted. But dwellings perhaps are still more insalubrious in those cottages situated at the backs of the houses fronting the street, the only entrance to which is through some nameless narrow passage, converted generally, as if by common consent, into a receptacle for ordure and the most offensive kinds of filth. The doors of these hovels very commonly open upon the uncovered cesspool, which receives the contents of the privy belonging to the house, and all the refuse cast out from it, as if it had been designedly contrived to render them as loathsome and unhealthy as possible. Surrounded on all sides by high walls, no current of air can gain access to disperse or dilute the noxious effluvia, or disturb the reeking atmosphere of these areas. Where there happens to be less crowding, and any ground remains unbuilt upon, it is generally undrained, contains pools of stagnant water, and is made a depot for dunghills and all kinds of filth.'

Considerations of factors such as the general environment, poor diet and the long term influence of mental, physical and moral squalor makes for an important dimension in the overall story of the factory children. Charles Dicken's description of the fictional 'Coketown' in his novel 'Hard Times', published in 1854, conveyed the soul-destroying nature of this environment; a "town of machinery and tall chimneys" with its "black canal and river that ran purple with the evil smelling dye." Dominating, was "the vast pile of building, full of windows, where there was a rattling and a trembling all day long where the piston of the steam engine worked monotonously up and down like the head of an elephant in a state of melancholy madness."

Having referred to some of the wider related issues, we can now consider the Ten Hour Day Movement and the process of reform from the early 1830s.

Michael Sadler, Tory M.P. for Leeds, was Chairman of the Select Committee on Factory Children's Labour and was also responsible for introducing a Ten Hours Bill in the House of Commons in 1831. From that time the Ten Hours Movement grew rapidly including amongst its members Anthony Ashley Cooper, later Lord Shaftsbury, Robert Owen, owner of the famous New Lanark Mills in Scotland, and John Fielden one of the most prominent manufacturers in the north of England. Robert Owen had demonstrated how it was possible to run his mills on a ten hour day and make a profit, yet also provide direct facilities – housing, schools, medical care, shops and goods for his workforce. No child was employed at New Lanark under the age of ten, and, instead, attended school. The New Lanark Mills did make for a model community but like all the enlightened employers of the day, Owen and Fielden recognised that voluntary efforts and example were not of themselves sufficient to bring about change.

The Ten Hours Bill aimed to secure reasonable working hours by law and when Ashley – (Lord Shaftsbury) took over the leadership of the movement after 1832 every effort was made to get the Bill through Parliament. Opponents to the Ten Hours Movement and to the various factory acts represented several points of view. Some objected to the idea of Parliament interfering in the manufacturing business; others pointed to the loss of profits which they claimed come with shorter hours. Sir Robert Peel argued against the Ten Hours Bill on the grounds that it was inadequate. He maintained that with some regulations on hours through Parliament more could be done for the factory worker by concentrating also on related matters such as public health and education and not merely hours alone as the Ten Hour Movement argued. Whilst he did not oppose restrictions on the hours of the working day generally, Peel did maintain that the actual ten hour day would be to the detriment of the working population itself. Setting out his case in opposition to the Ten Hours Bill of 1844 Peel claimed that it "must lead at a very early period to a great reduction in wages of workmen as it is vain to suppose that their Masters will give the same wages for ten hours as they gave for twelve."

The first disappointment for the Ten Hours Movement came in 1833. Following Sadler's Report, and a Royal Commission called by Parliament, the first effective factory legislation was passed. Not being, as the Factory Commissioners called them, "free agents," children were not in the position to choose for themselves regarding employment. It was accepted, therefore, that, unlike adults, able to make their own arrangements with employers, children needed protection.

Under the 1833 Act all children under the age of nine were to be banned from the mills; those from nine to thirteen years were to work a 48 hour week, whilst young people from thirteen to eighteen years were given a 69 hour week, and were banned from working at night. Each child was also to receive two hours schooling each day, developing the educational clause of the 1802 Act. Finally, and of great significance, was the appointment of four full time inspectors to enforce the Act. Their role was central to the gradual, overall improvement of conditions in the factories. They concerned themselves with a range of direct and related matters all directed to the benefit of the workforce. Concerns such as education, public health and questions of general safety all came under consideration.

Whilst the 1833 Act was not that anticipated by the Ten Hours supporters it did mark a decisive stage in the Factory Reform Movement. It became the model for later legislation and was most significant in terms of its potential. The actual details of the Act disappointed the supporters of the Ten Hour day, but the principle of government involvement had been established.

A view of Manchester from Kersall Moor, 1857. The contrast between the rural vantage point and the industrial landscape beyond was a characteristic feature of many Victorian illustrations. Numerous smoky chimneys testify to the concentrated manufacturing scene of Manchester, capital of the great cotton industry.

In its provision for education the Act was open to abuse. One of the most active and dedicated members of the Inspectorate, Leonard Horner, wrote of the weakness in the Act.

> The so-called education clauses enact no more than that the child shall attend a school; nothing is said as to the kind or quality of the education which they are to receive.

Included in one of the Inspector's later reports, at the mid century, are details of a number of would-be classrooms and the standards achieved.

> In this school there are 62 factory children. The master received an injury in a mill and therefore became a schoolmaster; he is evidently incompetent to teach more than the mere elements of instruction. The room is a wretched building, exposed on three sides, cold and damp.
>
> In this school 80 children were found crammed into a room 15 feet square. The master, wanting in ability and energy; the books, dirty; the room in a slovenly state, and used partly as a barber's shop.

Whilst the inspectors had the power to revoke a teacher's certificate when considered unfit they could not order that a school be established in a proper environment.

Further progress with factory reform came with the 1844 Act. In that year Parliament took another significant step by grouping women in the same category as young people, and, under the Act, reduced their working day to 12 hours. Children under 13 years were also limited to a working day of 6Å hours, but the minimum age for work was lowered a year, to 8. An important additional feature of the 1844 Act was the regulation that all dangerous machinery had to be fenced. This provision made the 1844 Act different from those preceding it. In legislating on actual working conditions it represented a new departure in the overall process of factory reform. A Select Committee of 1841 had investigated the question of safety in the factories. With ample evidence before them of maintenance work and cleaning being carried out whilst the machinery was in motion, and with numerous cases of accidents involving loss of life and limb, the Inspectorate was able to make a decisive improvement through the law.

Another valuable feature of the 1844 Act was its concern for the "half-time" system, whereby children divided their day between work and education. Where factory owners respected the Act and took it seriously the inspectors were able to report good results, but there were many cases of deliberate neglect or indifference to education. Parents might also obstruct the process, either from ignorance of the benefits of education or from desperate financial hardship. The possession of a valid certificate to show that a child had attended school could be gained from the employer's or parent's benefit without it actually having helped the child at all. Inspector Horner reported the following on the weakness of the system, pointing to the fact that many attendance certificates were worthless:

> 'It is very true that a large proportion of the children employed in factories who obtain certificates of attendance at a school, in fulfilment of the letter of the enactments in the Factory Acts, have received no instruction of any value – If the children are crammed into a cellar, and it is called a school, they must accept the certificates of their professed teacher. When such certificates are valid it is not to be wondered at if ignorant parents, unable to appreciate the value of education, send their children where they can obtain the legal qualification for employment at the least expense. Then, as to the employer of the child, in nine cases out of ten he looks no farther than to the possession of the legal certificate, and given himself no concern about the nature of the education.'

John Fielden's Ten Hour's Bill finally found favour with Parliament in 1847. Women and young persons had their hours limited to 11 in the first year, and 10 for the following. This legislation had the effect of limiting hours for men also, since they could not work effectively without assistance. A system of relays introduced for children made it possible, however, to keep men at work for much longer periods whilst restricting the child's movements and free time. Three years later the Factory Act of 1850 aimed to put a stop to the relays, but in doing so resulted in a revised 10½ hour day. A further Act of 1853 solved the problem.

During the second half of the century the main thrust of factory reform was with the extension of legislation to industries not covered by law. Cotton, wool, worsted, hemp, silk, flax and tow were the manufacturers covered by the Acts, but in 1861 children in the bleaching, dying and lace trades were included.

The Children's Employment Commission investigated a wide ranging number of trades during the 1860s and further Acts covered smaller workshops in 1867. Under a consolidating Act of 1878 all existing legislation was brought under a single Act drawing it together and codifying it under clear sections. This enabled the process of inspection to become far more efficient overall. No distinction now applied between a workshop and a factory.

From the mid 1870s onward the main thrust of improvement and progress came with the spread of elementary education. The Factory Act of 1878, Lord Sandon's Education Act of 1876 and the Mundella Act of 1880, marked important developments for children. The Mundella Act made elementary education compulsory to the age of 13, although children could leave school after the age of 10 providing that a valid certificate was produced indicating satisfactory standards of attendance and attainment.

Forster's Education Act of 1870 had brought the State into a far more active role in education. This allowed for the development of Board Schools where no Church school was available. Forster spoke of the Governments intention to 'fill up the gaps' in elementary education and emphasised that the State was not going into competition with the Church schools. The various religious denominations had fought for their own particular control over education and children with the result that they often actually prevented progress from fear of rivalry. This was the case in 1843 when attempts to improve educational opportunity for factory children were obstructed. 'Punch' produced several cartoons drawing attention to the effects of religious rivalry in matters of education. By 1870 considerable anxiety was expressed as to the condition of education, its overall provision and significance in the long-term development of Britain as a great industrial power. The State was obliged to take a direct role, but had to be sensitive to the various religious interests. School Boards were elected by local ratepayers and were responsible for the overall management of the school. The first board school to open was at Mount Charles, St. Austell in Cornwall, beginning classes in 1872. School attendance could only be made compulsory when sufficient accommodation had been provided.

The two Acts of 1876 and 1880, referred to above, made this possible. Thus, children were progressively removed from the sphere of employment into education, at least during their earlier years. Elementary education was made free of charge in 1891 and by the end of the century the school leaving age stood at 12.

Compulsory full-time education served to reveal the collective condition of children in the classroom. Gathered together in the schools their physical circumstances became clear to see. The ragged appearance, ill-health and inadequate diet of many children made it inevitable that a new stage in child care had to follow in the early twentieth century. The Liberal Government's work on behalf of children from 1906 to 1914 established the important link between education and welfare, which has grown rapidly to the present day. Their reforms also reflected an overall shift in emphasis and awareness of children's needs generally, building upon the slow but deliberate improvements of the past, as outlined here.

A 'Punch' cartoon of 1843. 'Substance and Shadow' carried the accompanying observation "Where one cannot give hungry nakedness the substance it covets, it shall have the shadow."

Chapter Two
Agricultural Life

North Lancashire

By the 1860s commercial and manufacturing interests in Lancashire accounted for 75 per cent of the population. With such a high proportion of the work force involved in cotton, coal, iron working etc. agricultural labour was much more scarce than elsewhere. The various industries paid higher wages than could normally be earned in farming, thus town life was more intense and characteristic of much of the county than was rural life. This often worked in favour of the agricultural labourer, however, as North Lancashire became one of the most prosperous parts of rural Britain for employer and employees alike.

Wages ranged from 16 to 18 shillings a week, well above the rates for southern counties such as Devon and Dorset where 8 to 10 shillings a week was quite common. The moral standards of the community generally were said to be comparatively high and were linked to the fact that female and child labour in the fields was scarce. Agricultural gangs, although widespread in Eastern England were 'entirely unknown', even in the Fylde district, which closely resembled the Lincolnshire Fens in its appearance and the type of farming.

Allotments and gardens were also noted for their high standard of cultivation. Potatoes, vegetables and flowers were plentiful whilst fruit trees were said to be 'common and highly prized'. A cottage without a good garden was considered the exception, and it was also estimated that in material terms such gardens, well maintained, were worth from £3 to £4 per year to the labourer. Summarising, the Assistant Commissioner wrote:

'The material condition of the agricultural labourer is satisfactory; there is little poverty and no distress; the general state of the rural population is one of prosperity and contentment.' The pastoral lands of the valley of the Lune, for example, constrasted with the reclaimed arable district of the Fylde. Both suffered from a shortage of labour which, in the former area, made arable farming almost impossible, even if desired. Two men could handle a farm of 600-800 acres, with wages offered at 18 shillings a week.'

A land steward in the Lune Valley contributed the following;

'Wages are so high and labour so scarce that we anxiously look to every improvement in machinery. We could not possibly save our hay without machines. Being myself a native of Devonshire, I tried to induce some labourers from the country who were only receiving 9 shillings a week to settle in this neighbourhood, where they received nearly double those wages; but after being a few months in the county they all returned to Devonshire. They missed their cider, and said they could not understand the Lancashire people, nor the Lancashire people them. Almost all our boys go off to the the manufacturing districts when they are 12 years of age, but they get a fair amount of education before that as there is nothing to interrupt it in the way of early labour.'

Labour was so scarce in the Fylde district that Irish immigrant labour became common. The Fylde was reclaimed land which, when drained and well manured, produced massive crops of potatoes. Land which had originally been worth as little as 5 shillings to 7 shillings and 6 pence fetched between 35 and 40 shillings when drained and improved. The Irish immigrant labour was seasonal, lasting from April to September.

Two examples of the conditions of life in the Fylde worth recording are those given by the Rev. Banister, vicar of Pilling, and Mr. W. Knowles, a farmer at Lytham.

In the first extract the Rev. Banister compared the district with that of the Lincolnshire Fenland. Whilst the two areas had detailed physical similarities with comparable crops and soils, the resemblance ended there, as will be seen in the next section:

'This part of Lancashire strongly resembles the Fens of Lincolnshire; it is reclaimed moss, and is now highly productive, growing potatoes, oats, wheat and beans. – Women are scarcely at all employed in outdoor work, but boys are required, chiefly for planting and gathering potatoes and in wheelings turfs to the carts for stacking. The school attendance is very good, one seventh of the population being under education. The employment boys get is no more than is good for them. In the winter months the school is very well attended, and at no season do we allow any child to continue absent without a satisfactory cause being shown.'

Mr. Knowles supported this overall picture. Whilst stating that without the assistance of Irish labour it would have been impossible to farm at all, this local farmer also commented on the lack of female labour in the fields. He also emphasised the facilities for education.

'The employment of women in field labour is scarcely known in this part of England, and boys are only occasionally employed, as in potato setting and wheeling turves to the stacks, a short period in Spring and Summer, leaving plenty of time for their education, for which the means are ample.'

Eastern Counties

Turning attention to Eastern England, considerable differences were apparent.

The Eastern Counties, as covered here, saw the widespread use of the 'Gang System'. Defining this method of work, the Commissioner on Children's Employment wrote:

'What is commonly understood by all as coming within the meaning of the term 'gang system' is where a person engages a number of workers, chiefly children and females, for the purpose of employing them in field work on the land of any farmer who may require his services, not being himself in the permanent service of any master, but following the business of overlooking such workers as an independent profession, and being hence known by the name of gangmaster or ganger.'

Large gangs which moved around the districts for hire were referred to as 'public gangs'. 'Private gangs' were also used, these being normally a more permanent workforce, directly

A delightful view of rural life as it was intended to be. An idyllic scene of peace, harmony and all the benefits of rural life has been offered here. Note the idealised, sentimental presentation of children taking part in Maytime celebrations.

employed by one farmer, with the ganger also being an employee of the farm.

The public gangs received most attention from the Commissioner as the scope for exploitation of the gang members was often greater. Gang sizes varied from groups as small as a dozen to much larger gatherings of up to fifty or so people. An average size gang was said to number from between twenty to twenty-five women and children. The farmers, it was said, preferred to employ women and children because the cost of their labour, from three to four shillings a week, was far less than that of an adult male labourer who earned between ten and eleven shillings weekly. Thus the gang system, whilst being an advantage to the farmer, made it difficult for men to find regular employment.

Gang work, a definitive feature of agricultural life in the Eastern Counties, had been in existence since the early years of the nineteenth century, but in many localities was estimated to be no more than 30 years old. Its existence at all was attributed to two main causes: the destruction of cottages in 'closed' parishes in order to avoid payment of poor rates, and, the enclosure and cultivation of former marsh or open land to make more farms. Whilst more land came into use, however, very few cottages were provided for the benefit of the working people, hence the long distances covered by the gangs to and from their work.

Before consideration of the gang system in general terms, it is useful to look at some first-hand accounts of this type of work and the numbers involved in a representative region. The table shows the approximate number of people working in gangs in the localities and parishes of the Lincolnshire Wolds, the Heath, Middle Fen and South Fen Districts, Northamptonshire, Huntingdonshire and Cambridgeshire.

Working conditions from women and children reflected the harsh nature of the gang system. In this first extract Elizabeth Dickson offered first-hand experience of such employment in Norfolk:

'Sometimes the poor children are very ill-used by the gangmaster. One has used them horribly, kicking them, hitting them with fork handles, handle sticks etc. and even knocking them down. I have many a time seen my own and other children knocked about by him in this way. It was not from drink, he was quite sober; but only because he was a masterless man. My children were obliged to go to work very young, some before they were seven years old. If you have nothing except

what comes out of your fingers' end, as they say, its no use, you must let them; they want more victuals. My husband left me a widow with eleven children living out of fifteen; none of them being then under sixteen years old, and three under three years, two being twins. The Parish allowed me 3s.4d. (16p) in many and goods (bread) according to the number of children, but not widow's pay. My Henry wasn't eight years old when I asked, "What will you turn him out"? They (the Parish) said, "well he's big enough, he must help as well as the others".

Jemima was not more than two months over six years old when she went out. She said, "Mother, I want some boots to go to school." So I sent her out and saved up what she earned till it was enough to get them, she was a corpse from going in the turnips. She comes home from work one day, when about 10½ years old, with dizziness and the bones aching, and died and was buried and all in little better than a fortnight. The doctor said it was a violent cold stuck in her bones. Children stooping down get as wet at top as below. They get wet from the rain too and come home so soaked that the wet will run out of their things. I have often obliged to take my flannel petticoat off and roll it round a girls legs and iron it with a warming pan to take off the pain and misery of the bones and let her get to sleep. When the gang goes far it tires the children much more and takes the shoes off the feet quicker, and they have to carry tools and extra victuals for the longer time, but have no more pay. Some of mine have gone four, five, six and seven miles off, and have gone from 6.30 am regular for a good time, and have not been home until seven or eight at night, or even later. Little ones at 6d., 5d., and 4d. a day have gone too. Some of the work is very hard, as pulling turnips and mangolds, much shaking, and when turnips are being put into the ground putting much as fast as the plough goes along – work which women and girls sometimes have to do. Drawing mangolds is the hardest; globe mangolds are fit to pull your insides out, and you often have to kick them up. I have pulled until my hands have been that swelled that you can't see the knuckles on them. I have come home so exhausted and I have sat down and cried; it would be an hour before I could pull my things off: and I have been obliged to have the table moved up to me because I could not move it.'

Sarah Ann Roberts also gave a graphic account of conditions in the gangs of Norfolk.

APPROXIMATE NUMBERS in the PUBLIC GANGS which were stated to go out from or to be employed in the following Parishes and Localities in Mr. LONGE'S District.

Numbers in the Public Gangs which go out:

In the Wolds:—
    From Caistor -   -   -   -   -   -   - 60
    ,,   Binbrooke - - - - - - 203
    ,,   Louth - - - - - - 120
In the Heath District - - - - - 60
In the Middle Fen District - - - - 180
In the South Fen District:
    From Spalding—
        In regular Gangs - - - 280 }
        In occasional Gangs - - 100 } 380
    ,,   Market Deeping }
    ,,   St. James's Deeping } - - - - 60
    ,,   Langtoft - - - - - 42
    ,,   Baston - - - - - 40
    ,,   Pinchbeck - - - - 30
    ,,   Crowland - - - - 100
    ,,   Bourn - - - - - 90
    ,,   Gedney Drove End - - - 40
                                  ——— 1405

Northamptonshire - - - - - - - 60

Huntingdonshire:
    From Yaxley - - - - - 161
    ,,   Stilton - - - - - 40
    ,,   Ramsey and R. }
    ,,   Ramsey St. John } - - - 220
    ,,   Warboys - - - - 60
    ,,   Somersham - - - - 50
                                  ——— 531

Cambridgeshire:
    From March - - - - - 388
    ,,   Doddington - - - - 222
    ,,   Benwick - - - - 65
    ,,   Chatteris - - - - 260
    ,,   Ely - - - - - 36
    ,,   Soham - - - - - 270
    ,,   Manea - - - - - 40
    ,,   Sutton - - - - - 40
    ,,   Wicken - - - - - 65
                                  ——— 1,386

In Mr. Longe's District - - - - - - - 3,382

NUMBER, SEX, and AGE of PERSONS employed in PUBLIC GANGS in or from the following (about 40) PARISHES in Mr. WHITE'S DISTRICT, as stated or estimated in the Returns.

| Parish or District. | Males. | | | | | Females. | | | | | | | Total Males and Females. |
| | Under 7. | Between 7 and 13. | Between 13 and 18. | Over 18. | Total Males. | Under 7. | Between 7 and 13. | Between 13 and 18. | Over 18. | | Total Females. | |
									Married.	Unmarried.		
NORFOLK.												
Tittleshall - -	—	7	3	—	10	—	6	5	3	1	15	25
Weasenham all Saints	—	3	—	—	3	—	15	5	7	—	27	*30
Great Dunham -	—	6	—	—	6	—	3	2	2	2	9	15
Grimston - -	—	15	15	—	30	—	15	15	3	2	35	65
Middleton - -	—	4	6	7	17	—	4	2	16	3	25	42
Welney - -	—	20	10	—	30	—	10	20	20	—	50	80
Hilgay - -	—	7	—	—	7	—	5	—	7	4	16	23

Contemporary scenes of rural life showing harvest time and a farmyard view.

'Soon I went out with the gang, when I was eleven perhaps, I got the rheumatism. The work was so wet; we have been dripping through, especially in wheat. When low it would be up to our knees, and sometimes it was up to our shoulders; we have weeded it when in the ear. I have been so wet that I have taken off my clothes and wrung them out and hung them up to dry on the top of some wheat or anywhere while we went in again to weed. We durst not hang up only light things such as aprons, handkerchiefs, etc. not petti-coats. We have had to take off our shoes and pour the water out, then the man would say, "now then, go on again". Often when it came on to rain there was no shelter within reach, but, if there was any, sometimes he would not let us go till we were drenched. I often blame him for making my bones sore. I have great pain, and when you came in just now began to tremble fearing it was another doctor at me. My knee is so bad, and nearly as big as a loaf, but I have to keep moving it about for ease. I can only go with a crutch and stick.'

Walking to and from the place of work was quite separate from the actual day's labour itself. Mrs. Anthony Adams, a labourer's wife from Denton in Huntingdonshire de-scribed the distances covered by her daughters:

'In June 1862, my daughters, Harriet and Sarah, aged respectively 11 and 13 years, were engaged by a ganger to work on Mr. Worman's land at Stilton. When they got there he took them on to Peterborough; there they worked for six weeks, going and returning each day. The distance each way is eight miles, so that they had to walk sixteen miles a day, on all six working days of the week, besides working in the field from 8 am to 5 or 5.30 in the afternoon. They used to start from home at 5 in the morning and seldom got back before 9. Sometimes they were put to hoeing, sometimes to twitching and they had 7d. a day. They had to find all their own meals as well as their own tools. They (the girls) were good for nothing at the end of six weeks.'

Together with the obvious physical hardship of field work the gang system was also said to encourage immorality amongst the young people. They were away from home for long periods of time and lacked the appropriate supervision of parents or any responsible adult. Moreover, the mixed gangs gave easy and familiar proximity between the boys and girls.

In one example, in Downham in Norfolk, the curate related how at harvest time one gang of children left their homes on the Monday morning only to return on the following Saturday night. They slept together in a barn provided by the farmer. The curate also emphasised that this was not an unusual practice when the gangs had a great distance to travel.

Dr. Morris of Spalding, the Medical Officer to Spald-ing Union Infirmary stated that the gang system was largely the reason for indecent behaviour amongst the young people. In correspondence to the Childrens Employment Commission he wrote:

'I am convinced that the gang system is the cause of much immorality. The evil in the system is the mixture of the sexes, in this case, of boys and girls of 12 to 18 years of age under no proper control. The gangers take the work of the farmers. Their custom is to pay the children once a week at some beer house and it is no uncommon thing for those children to be waiting at the place until 11 or 12 o'clock at night. At the infir-mary many girls of 14 and even of 13, up to 17 years of age have been brought in and confined there. The girls have acknowledged that their ruin has taken place in this gang work. I once saw a young girl insulted by some five or six boys on the road side. Other older persons were about 20 or 30 yards off, but they took no notice. The girl was calling out which caused me to stop. I have seen boys bathing in the brooks and girls between 13 and 19 years of age looking on from the bank.'

The reference to young girls' confinement in the work-houses was supported by several other reports. In one instance, a union official reported that the same girls re-turned for second or even third confinements as a result of working in the gangs. Cases of boys and girls bathing together or watching one another were also common.

Parental supervision was extremely limited, and fre-quently non existent. In certain cases adults would live together, outside marriage, raising several children "ignor-ant in every respect of decency, morality and religion". The Boards of Guardians in an attempt to prevent couples simply living together cut off any financial support where this situation applied.

Conditions were not always better when the parents were married. Women who worked in the gangs were considered generally to make poor housewives whilst their daughters were held to be unemployable in any other type of work once they had been in the gangs. It was stated that they grew rough and course in manner and were quite unfit to become household servants or reasonable wives and mothers themselves. According to the rector of one East Anglian parish:

'To say that a girl had been employed in the fields, in gangs or otherwise, is generally sufficient to cause anyone above the class of the smaller farmers and tradesmen to reject her.'

Describing the effect of the gang system on one village in Norfolk during the recent fast the correspondent to the Commissioner called the community 'a sink of wickedness'. He reported how no female could walk through the streets without being insulted and told one farmer's wife who was afraid to come to church on account of 'the indecent and improper language addressed to her by idle lads and boys assembled at the different corners'. Continuing his criticism of village conditions the correspondent wrote:

'Obscene and indecent expressions were written in chalk on the walls; lads, and almost boys, were seen drunk in the village street; drunkenness and swearing were common amongst the men; many of the women were or had been unchaste; the church was neglected and the Sunday was spent by the men and lads in all kinds of riotous sports and pastimes.'

One of the greatest encouragements to immorality was widely recognised in the appalling conditions of cottage accommodation. Hopelessly overcrowded, insanitary, and lacking in almost all domestic comforts the labourers' cot-tages were criticised in this and many other parts of Britain. In describing the worst type of accommodation in Norfolk the Commissioner told of a cottage which he considered

The Hay Harvest.

to be no more than, 'a hovel about 12 feet by 9 feet 6 inches and the door, which reached nearly to the top of the wall was not 5 feet 6 inches high, with thatched roof bare inside, and with no outdoor accommodation.' Such a place with only its single room served as living and sleeping area for an entire family of up to eight people.

In attending a child dying from typhoid fever the Medical Officer of Spalding Union reported that a family of ten people had to share the cottage's only bedroom. The entire family had no alternative to that of remaining in the room with the child and when he eventually died there was, again, no option but to keep the body there until the time of burial.

Looking to improvements in childrens' lives at the time it was considered essential to regulate the working of the gang system. Robert Everard, writing on Lincolnshire, argued that to prohibit the labour of children would be to prohibit the proper cultivation of the land. He emphasised the extreme financial hardships involved in any attempt to ban young people from useful employment and recognised their important contribution to agricultural work. He did, however, offer the following recommendations. Firstly, that the boys and girls should not be employed in the same gangs; secondly, that boys should not begin work before the age of ten, and the girls before the age of eleven; thirdly, that there should be fixed hours of work, which he suggested as 7.30 am to 5 pm with an hour's break for dinner.

Such recommendations indicate that the main concern was with controlling and regulating the conditions of gang work. There was no reference to children being removed from work completely.

Together with such regulations, it was also seen important to actively promote education within the community. Whilst education remained voluntary, however, and with a recognised shortage of schools to take them, children often had little real opportunity of receiving any sustained education likely to benefit them. In many cases even where and when school could be attended, it was a financial impossibility for large numbers of would-be pupils. Children were an essential part of the rural workforce, a fact recognised by the Royal Commission on Education in 1861:

> 'At particular seasons the population is not more than sufficient to do the work and frequently the whole number of available hands is required at once.'

It was, in fact, legislation on education which brought about the end of child labour in the agricultural gangs. The Gang Act of 1868 banned the employment of children under eight years of age, introduced licenced gang mistresses for women and girls and compelled gang masters to hold a licence themselves. It was the Education Acts of 1876 and 1880, however, introducing compulsory education that eventually had the greatest impact.

Dorset

Child labour, both male and female, was particularly widespread in Dorset. The accompanying table, based on the census of 1851 and 1861, reveals that in the seven sample counties included, Kent, Chester, Shropshire, Staffordshire, Rutland and Lincolnshire – the greatest number of young people at work were clearly to be found in Dorset.

TABLE, founded on the Census of 1851 and 1861, to show the comparative Employment of Juvenile and Female Labour in the under-mentioned Counties.

Counties.		Male Agricultural Labourers.		Between 5 and 10.	Between 10 and 15.	Percentage under 15.	Female Agricultural Labourers.		Under 15.
Kent	1851	Outdoor	41,462	143	3,549	8¼	520		51
		Indoor	4,994	4	254		1,756		140
	1861	Outdoor	43,186	163	3,604	8	589		50
		Indoor	3,698	3	352		252		14
Dorset	1851	Outdoor	19,302	232	2,327	13	1,919		144
		Indoor	602	1	72		1,293		111
	1861	Outdoor	19,070	271	2,397	14	1,413		95
		Indoor	364	2	80		689		39
Chester	1851	Outdoor	14,296	6	488	7	316		12
		Indoor	7,279	15	929		1,496		173
	1861	Outdoor	16,861	11	526	7	315		12
		Indoor	6,452	4	1,063		1,513		61
Salop	1851	Outdoor	18,851	48	822	9	328		10
		Indoor	7,593	16	1,216		1,934		168
	1861	Outdoor	18,288	15	593	8	412		8
		Indoor	7,389	21	1,463		1,632		15
Stafford	1851	Outdoor	18,556	28	716	6	455		19
		Indoor	5,770	6	766		984		32
	1861	Outdoor	18,494	43	935	8	412		12
		Indoor	4,629	13	883		1,316		30
Rutland	1851	Outdoor	2,486	5	195	9	8		—
		Indoor	409	2	49		6		—
	1861	Outdoor	2,911	14	254	9	10		6
		Indoor	339	1	26		127		8
Lincoln	1851	Outdoor	39,810	127	3,080	8	389		53
		Indoor	10,878	5	769		769		57
	1861	Outdoor	42,984	211	3,669	9	729		104
		Indoor	9,897	8	843		3,477		249

An idealised portrait of Dorsetshire farmworkers from the mid 1840s.

Evidence from communities such as Sturminster Marshall in East Dorset and Marnhull, in the north of the county, reflect a common practice whereby children began work at a very early age.

The Rev. Kegan Paul, vicar of Sturminster Marshall summarised:

'Few of the boys stay at the day school after 8. The majority begin farm labours at that age, some much earlier, even at 5 years old.'

His evidence from 1868, also included a list of thirteen children (boys) drawn from five families giving the ages at which they began regular work. Their ages varied between 5 and 10 years, their's being a representative example from the community generally, but not including those families in the greatest poverty, or those whose condition was the result of recklessness.

Poverty was given as the root cause of such early labour amongst children, eight to ten shillings a week being the common wage level in Dorset. This was not the only reason, however. In many cases evidence was given that the employing farmers insisted on young children working as a condition to giving work to the father. Similar conditions also applied to wives. When two boys from a family could be brought to work it would often save the expense of an able-bodied adult, the children being cheap to employ. Thus labourers with large families could prove an attractive proposition to their prospective employer.

The schoolmistress at the National School in Marnhull related similar circumstances for that community during the late 1860s:

TABLE showing the age at which Boys and Girls leave School in Parishes in Dorset.

	Boys.	Girls.
Whitechurch - (Certificated master and mistress.)	10, maximum -	14 or 15. In some cases a little knitting done.
Milborne St. Andrew. (Mistress.)	10, maximum -	Rather later.
Durweston - (Mistress.)	9 or 10. Irregular from 8.	13.
Milton Abbas -	9. Work begins at 7 or 8 for many of them.	——
Stourpaine - - (Certificated mistress.)	- - -	10 or 11 sometimes, on account of the knitting and gloving.
Pimperne - (Certificated master and mistress.)	" Very unusual to keep them after 10."	12 or 13. A little gloving.
Hilton - (Certificated master and mistress.)	10 or 11, maximum	Some girls leave before 10. " Gloving" common.
Langton - Tarrant Gunville -	} No schools.	
Spettisbury and Charlton. (Free school.)	Average, 9. Some begin work at 6 or 7.	About 11.
Sturminster Marshall.	8, maximum. In November only six in school were over 7.	——

A labourer's cottage near Blandford, Dorset, 1846. This particular view expresses, in part, the attraction of rural life to the town dweller, but the observation of the writer in the Illustrated London News was appropriate; "This is a charmingly picturesque bit for the painter; though its propped-up walls and decaying thatched roof, too closely indicate the privation and suffering of the inmates."

'I have no boys now in my school over 8 years old, and no girls over 10. There are so many farmers here employing boys that they get work very young. Some will go out for one shilling a week to bird minding. Men who work on the farms will get their lads to go when very young. One boy in my school went bird-keeping when he was not much over 4 years old. A good many go at 6 and 7. I had a boy in my school between 8 and 9 who was getting on nicely, and now he has gone off turkey-keeping and I hear he is not to come back. Lots of them who leave in this way can scarcely write at all. Just as they begin to learn they are taken away.

The girls leave to go gloving. Little girls of 6 and 7 can do something. Even before they leave altogether they are very irregular, the parents wanting them for one cause or another; and then when they get to 8 or 9 years they are rather ashamed of the little they learn, and wont come any more.'

The accompanying table shows the age at which boys and girls left school in Dorset generally. Cottage accommodation in Dorset was investigated and reported by several sources during the 1840s. The hopelessly overcrowded and insanitary homes were frequently criticised for being no more than sources of misery and immorality. Influential documents such as Edwin Chadwick's famous 'Report on the Sanitary condition of the Labouring Population' of 1842 and the 'Report on the Employment of Women and Children in Agriculture' of 1843 focused attention on the subject. 'The Illustrated London News' of September 1846 also gave detailed coverage of the conditions of rural life in certain Dorset Villages.

The evidence of Mr. John Foxe, Medical Officer of Cerne Union, offered an accurate picture of cottage accommodation at its worst. His investigations were included in Chadwick's Sanitary Report of 1842, representing Dorset:

'I have often seen the springs bursting through the mud floor of some of the cottages, and little channels cut from the centre under the doorways to carry off the water, whilst the door has been removed from its hinges for the children to put their feet on whilst employed in making buttons. It is not surprising that fever and scrofula in all its forms prevail under such circumstances. Most of the cottages being of the worst description, some mere mud hovels, and situated in low and damp places with cesspools or accumulations of filth close to the doors. The mud floors of many are much below the level of the road and in wet seasons are little better than so much clay. In many of the cottages, also, where synochus prevailed, the beds stood on the ground floor, which was damp three parts of the year; scarcely one had a fireplace in the bedroom, and one had a small pane of glass stuck in the mud as its only window, with a large heap of wet and dirty potatoes in one corner. Persons living in such cottages are generally very poor, very dirty, and usually in rags, living almost wholly on bread and potatoes, scarcely ever tasting animal food, and consequently highly susceptible to disease and very unable to contend with it.'

In sharp contrast with the view of the rural world as it was often imagined, conditions of village life were invariably very different. The two scenes here of outdoor and indoor life in Dorset, reflect circumstances very similar to those experienced by town dwellers in as far as housing and matters of basic public health were concerned. Whilst the virtues and beneficial effects of country life were praised in both literature and art, rural society had a harsh reality.

The 'Royal Commission on the Employment of Children, Young Persons and Women in Agriculture of 1867 reported on Cerne Abbas 25 years later. One and two bedroomed cottages were still numerous throughout the surrounding district and in Cerne Abbas itself the passage of time had brought little improvement, if any. The cottages were thus described:

'Very poor, most of them thatched, there is scarcely one with three bedrooms, most have two, but the separation is very often indifferent indeed. Rooms in most cases very low, hardly six feet and the windows are very often not made to open. In some cases only one privy to five in six cottages. The drains are very bad; the water supply good.'

Evidence from the 'Report on Women and Children in Agriculture 1843' highlighted the chronic overcrowding at Stourpaine. In the report carried out by the Poor Law authorities a cottage bedroom in the village was described as 10 feet square, the middle of the room being seven feet high. There was a fireplace and one window about 15 inches square. In this room there were three beds. One was occupied by the father, mother, a small child 1½ years old, and an infant of four months. Three sisters slept in the second bed, twins aged 20 and a younger girl aged 7. The third bed was for the four sons aged 17, 15, 14 and 10 years. Given such conditions it came as no surprise that the cottages were regarded as 'fruitful sources of misery and immorality'.

The Illustrated London News of September 1846 also focused on village life in Dorset. Drawing on material from the Times Correspondent the community of Stourpaine was again considered:

'The first feature which attracts the attention of the stranger on entering the village is the total want of cleanliness which pervades it. A stream composed of matter which constantly escapes from the pigsties and other receptacles of filth meanders down each street, being here and there collected into standing ponds which lie festering and rotting in the sun and so create wonder that the place is not the continual abode of pestilence – indeed the worst malign fevers have raged here at different times. It may be sufficient to add for the present that the inside of the cottages in every respect correspond with the external appearance of the place.'

To conclude this section it is worth referring to two further points. The first was the statement from the Times Correspondent as to the reason for such conditions: 'In no County' he wrote, 'notwithstanding the universal increase in population, is the want of new cottages so apparent, and the neglect of the landlord, in this point at least, so con-

spicuous.' The second and final point is to note that Lord Shaftsbury's father, the sixth Earl, owned property in the village of Stourpaine. This fact, of course, was not lost to Ashley's opponents and made for interesting irony when considering his work on behalf of factory reform in the north of England.

Widespread poverty, excessive labour, inferior accommodation and diet were obvious features of rural life bearing directly upon children's fortunes. Being dependants, their circumstances were inevitably linked to those of their parents, thus for the community overall, adult and child, there were considerable problems. By way of further reference, this time to Oxfordshire and Herefordshire, one can examine the attempt to actually confront one of the most important issues affecting children's lives, namely the conflicting demands of education and employment. This specific question encompassed all other existing problems mentioned here in one way or another, relating to every individual and community alike.

The Swyncoombe Industrial School, (1846) a corrective establishment giving custodial training, and the Watlington Training School for girls (1865) performed useful functions within their immediate rural location, but both had potential reference beyond, into the agricultural community at large.

As founder of the Swyncoombe School the Rev. Keene argued that it was possible to resolve the conflict between education and work and that the means existed to do so. Obstacles to education were considered greater in the countryside than in the towns but a structured combination of education and work might offer a solution. Recognising parental indifference and the hostility of many farmers at the loss of ready labour, the Rev. Keene argued:

'There are not wanting examples to show that under favourable circumstances, the combination of labour and mental learning may be adopted with advantage, and that children may be enabled, as a sort of apprentices, to fit themselves for their future work as comfortably skilled labourers when they leave school. In all cases of popular education I am of the opinion that there should be a mixture of manual employment with the mental training. It relieves the irksome sameness of elementary education through the day, and in so doing allows the mind during its shorter period of tensions to be more capable of digesting its lessons. The bodily exercise and incipient Fitness for employment will always be found advantageous to the child's future career.'

Healthy exercise and mental application was, of course, a combination endorsed by the public school of the day. The latter, encouraged sport for character and exercise, whilst

Ages.	North-western Counties (Cheshire, &c.).		South-western (Dorset, &c.).		District of Wimborne (Dorset).		District of Sherborne (Dorset).	
	Males.	Females.	Males.	Females.	Males.	Females.	Males.	Females.
All ages	2·674	2·433	2·072	1·936	1·818	1·827	2·032	2·018
Under 5	9·366	8·203	5·634	4·867	4·923	3·782	6·213	5·116
5	1·054	1·005	·724	·764	·552	·552	·667	·834
10	·568	·538	·438	·494	·413	·443	·463	·502
15	·792	·816	·559	·677	·541	·820	·456	·760
25	·923	·908	·883	·798	·753	1·110	·731	·737
35	1·033	1·114	·932	·890	·815	·956	·756	1·006
45	1·455	1·437	1·101	1·024	·980	1·262	·957	1·197
55	2·210	1·950	1·532	1·255	1·117	1·195	1·304	1·298
65	3·809	3·386	2·738	2·302	2·260	2·482	2·607	2·337
75	7·803	7·101	5·854	5·301	4·886	4·894	5·714	5·263
85 and upwards	16·338	14·878	13·747	12·937	12·308	14·338	13·402	15·487
	31·828	29·986	30·959	28·799	24·583	23·214	30·000	31·053

Table showing the comparative annual mortality for 1851-61 in various districts.

One of a series of agricultural pictures from the mid century showing thrashing work in the barn.

working children were to apply themselves to physical work, thus was posed another of Victorian England's interesting ironies whereby the rugger field and the hayfield respectively, seemed to embrace something of a common purpose.

Developing his proposals, Rev. Keene emphasised that compulsory education could not be seriously contemplated, "unless tempered by some plan of relief from the effects of loss of the child's earnings when at school".

'If compulsory education is to be enforced, the manual labour which may be made part of the school business should be of a remunerative character so that the child or its parents may participate in its results.'

To apply the principles and pattern of education as followed in the industrial schools, minus their custodial corrective ethos, would serve to greatly enhance educational provision in rural areas where, otherwise, not formal structure existed. Education had become a dimension of factory life in textile manufacturers but nothing comparable applied in agriculture, often the most lowly paid sector of society.

The Rev. Keene's Industrial School provided for supervised employment on the land, and an element of active training in workshops, whilst it also emphasised formal learning – reading, writing, geography, history, etc. Working on the half-day principle from Monday to Saturday, time was shared between school work and practical employment. Thus a variant on the half-day pattern in industry was offered, perhaps evisaging a set number of hours or days for education and, others, for work. Evidence

from Wiltshire, the Rev. W. Brodribb, of Wootton Rivers, also supported this introduction of the half-time system as the only way to achieve compulsory education.

In Herefordshire, the Rev. W. Poole, Secretary to the County Diocesan Board of Education, emphasised the problems for compulsory education:

'There exists a very strong feeling against cumpulsory education. It is reckoned an interference with private life; it is thought likely to augment pauperism, it is considered to be unworkable; it is hard on the farmers who want hands; it is hard on the parents who want money. Any law simply exacting that all children shall be educated would be likely to meet a general opposition and that neglect or indifference which is even harder to contend against than actual opposition itself.'

The Rev. Poole put forward a specific four-point plan which he argued should be taken in conjunction with the attempt to foster compulsory education, making it far more acceptable. His plan also underlines the independent nature of the education issue, the four main areas within his scheme being:

1. Securing decent and sufficient dwellings for the poor.
2. Providing against sickness and old age.
3. Providing recreation and instruction for elder lads/men.
4. The requirement that all children should be educated to a certain standard.

Children under 12 years should possess a licence to indicate a necessary level of education and masters were not to employ children who did not present such proofs of their ability. Having put forward these proposals, however,

'An English goldfield!' A cartoon from 'Punch', July 1852, underlines the prosperous and healthy circumstances of English agriculture during what was known as the golden age of farming. The title was also a reference to the activities of those at work in the goldfields overseas, and the tremendous attention focused upon it. 'Punch' presented this cartoon, emphasising prosperity and wealth at home alongside a less salutary scene of prospectors at work in New South Wales and Victoria, South Australia. The safe, cosy and contented image offered here, complete with children at leisure and the boy bird scaring, hid the fact that despite the good fortunes in agriculture overall, the labouring community derived little positive improvement themselves.

the Rev. Poole were well aware that the active cooperation of all concerned with a commitment to education would be imperative for their success. This much was acknowledged.

> 'The half time system has been successfully carried out in special instances, but in every case I believe where this has occurred among our agricultural population it has been owing to the active intervention of some influential individual who has given his time and often his money to work it out, otherwise it seems unlikely that this plan would succeed.'

Whilst the Rev. Poole's proposals envisaged features of the programme of radical reform implemented by the Liberal Government of 1906-1914, the problems confronting him in the 1860s reflected the circumstances of Robert Owen and the factory reform movement some forty years earlier, leading into the 1830s.

Returning to the example of Oxfordshire, a final reference to the Watlington Training School also reflected developments somewhat akin to the coal mining communities. This training school for girls offered opportunities, albeit on a small scale, for girls in the rural districts to become household servants. Like the Walkden Manor School for colliery girls, near Manchester, the Oxfordshire school took some ten to twelve girls preparing them for employment. Under the control of the Counties of Macclesfield, the staff fostered self-sufficiency, reliability and order.

'The girls keep the whole building clean and in order. They bake their own bread, cook their own food and cure their bacon, make and mend their clothes. Laundrywork is the chief occupation.'

Spare time during the afternoon or evening was devoted to reading, writing, needlework, arithmetic and a degree of religious instruction. Entry to the Watlington Training School took place between the ages of 12 and 16, 14 being the most desirable. Pupils attended the school for a period of one to three years duration according to age, proficiency and strength. It was also expected that all applicants should be able to read and write on admission.

The Watlington School was founded on clear vocational principles and its relationship to general education and schools was not as immediate as the proposals set out by the churchmen from Oxfordshire and Herefordshire. That it excited at all was, however, was evidence for an element of progress and opportunity, over and against considerable rural deprivation.

In as far as they confronted the more serious issues of rural life the experience and example of these various interests in Oxfordshire and Herefordshire helped to contributed to an overall perspective on life in rural Britain. Their attempts to not only describe events and issues but to work towards a solution reflected their obvious appreciation of the nature and scope of the problems. Looking back, we can only gain from their debate, regardless of its outcome at that time.

'Harvest Home' – a mid century illustration.

Chapter Three
The Coal Industry

Coal was the life-blood of nineteenth century industry. From the leading manufacturing interests nationally, right down to small local concerns, there was an absolute reliance upon regular coal supplies to meet both the existing and increasing demands of trade. The rapidly expanding railway network of the early Victorian years, itself an important consumer, made it possible to distribute coal rapidly, reliably and cheaply to ever widening markets. Canals and coastal shipping were also important to the development of trade, whilst an active and extremely valuable export business again encouraged further investment.

Looking across a century of development, the production figures for the coal industry speak for themselves. From an estimated 10/11 million tons in 1800 production rose to a fraction below 50 million tons in 1850 and to a record output of 287 million tons in 1913.

Progress in the coalfields during the late eighteenth and early nineteenth centuries was linked to the capacity to solve certain fundamental technical problems. Drainage, lighting, ventilation and the related danger of explosion from pockets of gas within the coal seams each presented obstacles to progress, and, collectively, threatened to put severe limitations upon the expansion through deep mining. By the 1840s these problems had been largely resolved but mining always remained a highly dangerous occupation offering no basis for complacency from any quarter. Steam pumps vastly improved ventilation techniques and the con-

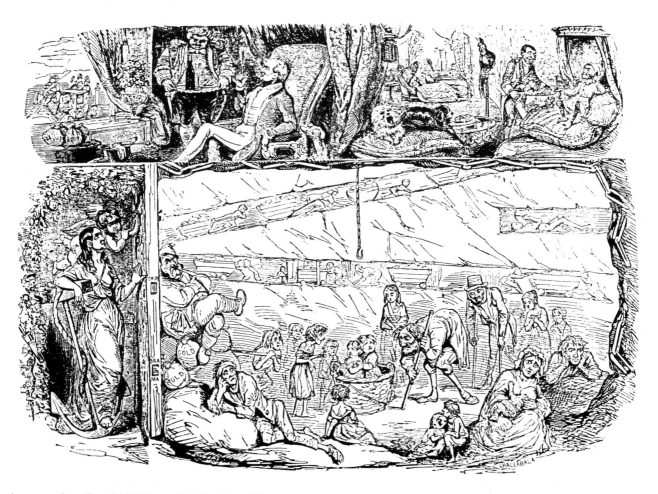

A cartoon from 'Punch', 1843 entitled 'Capital and Labour.' Like the earlier example, also drawing on comparison, contrast and irony (substance and shadow), the riches and luxury derived from coal are apparent here, and set as intended, in sharp contrast with the labours of those underground. 'Punch' offers a darker interpretation developing simple contrast: "When taken in conjunction with these very pleasing pictures, (the scenes of affluence) the labourers in the mines must have had a very different aspect from that which injudicious writers have endeavoured to attach to them. The works being performed wholly underground ought never to have intruded on the notice of the public." In fact, the reports, and especially the illustrations, of life in the mines from 1842 directed great attention on work in the mines. Despite the opposition of many coal-labourers, Parliament was, for once, shocked at the findings of the commission, and acted swiftly, although its concern was primarily with moral conditions rather than the extensive physical exploitation in itself.

tribution of the 'Davy' and 'Geordie' lamps played a decisive part in opening up the coalfields in the earlier decades of the nineteenth century, enabling the coal industry to make its unique contribution to the Victorian economy.

Whilst a great deal of time, expertise and investment was successfully directed towards the problems of winning the coal, the actual workforce was, by comparison, the subject of conspicuous neglect. Their working conditions were, for the most part, desperately inadequate as the following chapter should reveal. Men, women and children risked their lives on a daily basis in the mines and it was not until 1842 that the first effective steps were taken by government to intervene on their behalf. As the entire content of this book will show, progress was invariably slow and, then, only gained at great cost.

The Coal Mines

The 'Reports to the Commissioners on the Employment of Children' 1842, gave a graphic account of the conditions of work in the coal mines. As Sub-Commissioner reporting on Lancashire, J. L. Kennedy was forthright in some of his conclusions about conditions in the mines:

'No argument is necessary to convince a person who has witnessed females at work in the mines, that it is an employment very ill-suited to their sex.'
Reporting on the collieries of East Scotland R H Franks also condemned the use of women and children describing their situation as being no better than 'base feudalism' and 'cruel slavery':

'It is revolting to humanity to reflect upon the barbarous and cruel slavery which this degrading labour constitutes. An employment which, from the manner in which it is still conducted, may be regarded a relic of base feudalism, and which in the nineteenth century continues to excite our disgust and compassion.'
The outcome of the Report was legislation in Parliament to ban women and girls from the mines completely and to prohibit the employment of boys below the age of 10. Introduced into the House of Commons by Anthony Ashley Cooper (Lord Shaftesbury) on 7 June 1842, the Miners Bill became law that year bringing to an end a situation considered by many people to be a national disgrace and humiliation in a Christian country.

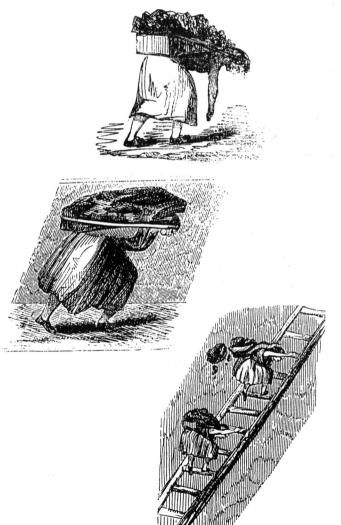

Average Net Weekly Earnings of the different Classes of Operatives in the Cotton Factories of Manchester, Stockport, Duckenfield, Staleybridge, Hyde, Tintwistle, Oldham, Bolton, &c., drawn from the returns of 151 mills, employing 48,645 persons, in May, 1833:—

Denomination of Process in which employed.	Class of Operatives.	Classification as respects Age and Sex.	Average Weekly Net Earnings.	
			s.	d.
Cleaning and spreading cotton	. . . . .	Male and female adults, and some non-adults . . .	8	3
Carding . . .	Carders or overlookers	Male adults . . .	23	6
	Jack-frame tenters .	Principally female adults . . .	8	0
	Bobbin-frame tenters	Do. do. . .	7	5½
	Drawing tenters . .	Do. do. . .	7	5¼
Mule-spinning .	Overlookers . . .	Male adults . . .	29	3
	Spinners . . .	Male and female adults, but principally the former .	25	8
	Piecers	Male and female adults and non-adults, but principally the letter .	5	4½
	Scavengers . . .	Male and female non-adults . . .	2	10½
Throstle-spinning . .	Overlookers . .	Male adults . . .	22	4½
	Spinners . . .	Female adults and non-adults . .	7	9
Weaving . . .	Overlookers . . .	Male adults . . .	26	3½
	Warpers . . .	Male and female adults . . .	12	3
	Weavers . . .	Male and female adults, male and female non-adults, but chiefly females	10	10
	Dressers	Male adults . . .	27	9½
Reeling . . .	Reelers	Female adults and non-adults . .	7	11½
Roller covering	Roller coverers .	Male and female adults	12	1¼
Attending the steam-engine, and making machines . .	Engineers, firemen, mechanics, &c.	Male adults . . .	20	6

* Supplementary Report of the Factory Commissioners, part i. pp. 124-5. Supplements B and E.

Girls were also employed to carry coal from the face workings to the shafts and from one level to another. The three illustrations here reflect the hardship and dangers involved.

Female labour was not a feature of every coalfield. Many districts opposed it completely and even where it was found within a particular field, certain mines or districts refused to take women and girls. Those districts where female labour was banned included South Staffordshire, North Staffordshire, Shropshire, Warwickshire, Leicestershire, Derbyshire, Oldham (Lancashire), Cumberland, Durham and Northumberland, North Wales, Forest of Dean, South Gloucestershire and North Somerset.

Of the coalfields employing women underground, the highest proportion was found in the Pembrokeshire district of West Wales and in Eastern Scotland. The Lancashire, Yorkshire and Glamorgan coalfields also employed women and girls. Female employment in West Scotland was described as 'extremely rare, but not entirely unknown'. The accompanying table shows the proportion of females to males employed below ground.

Proportion (nearly) of Females to adult Males, and of Females under age to Males under age.

Districts.	Adults.	From 13 to 18.	Under 13.
Yorkshire	1 to 45	1 to 25	1 to 25
Lancashire	1 to 12	1 to 13	1 to 37
East of Scotland:			
Mid Lothian	1 to 3	1 to 5½	1 to 20
East Lothian	1 to 3	1 to 3½	1 to 10
West Lothian	1 to 5	1 to 7	1 to 10
Stirlingshire	1 to 4½	1 to 8	1 to 10
Clackmannanshire	1 to 5	1 to 5	1 to 11½
Fifeshire	1 to 5½	1 to 10	1 to 30
Wales:			
Glamorganshire	1 to 53	1 to 53	1 to 83
Pembrokeshire	1 to 2½	1 to 8½	1 to 53

Together with detailed descriptions of the work in the mines, the Report of 1842 also included a large number of illustrations showing men, women and children at work. This had the effect of highlighting the wretched nature of the work, and helped considerably in the movement to 'ban' female labour below ground.

In his coverage of the collieries of East Scotland, R H Franks included the evidence of Janet Cumming, an 11 year old coal-bearer. Her work was typical of the large number of women and girls employed:

'I gang with the women at five and come up at five at night; work all night on Fridays and come away at twelve in the day. I carry the large bits of coal from the wallface to the pit bottom, and the small pieces called chows to the creel. The weight is usually a hundred-weight; do not know how many pounds there are in a hundredweight, but it is Some weight to carry; it takes three journeys to fill a tub of four hundred-weight. The distance varies as the work is not always on the same wall; sometimes 150 fathoms, whiles 250 fathoms. The roof is very low; I have to bend my back and legs and the water comes frequently up to the calves of my legs. Have no liking for the work; father makes me like it. Never got hurt, but often obliged to scramble out of the pit when bad air was in'.

Two further examples from East Scotland cover other forms of work, namely 'putting and pumping'. 'Putting' was the task of pulling loaded waggons of coal from the working place to the horse-roads, and was then taken to the shafts by others.

Jane Moffat was a coal-putter, 12 years of age. Her hours were given as from 6 am to 6 pm with a night shift on alternate weeks:

'I pull the waggons of 4 to 5 hundredweight from the men's rooms (working areas) to the horse-road. We are worse off than the horses as they draw on iron rails, and we on the flat floors. We have no meals below. Some of us get pieces of bread when we can save it from the rats, who are so ravenous that they eat the corks out of our oil-flasks. I draw the carts through the narrow seams. The roads are 24 to 30 inches high; draw in harness, which passes over my shoulders and back; and the cart is fastened to my chain. The place of work is very wet and covers my shoe-top. I work on mother's account, with sister, as father was killed in the pit five years since. These are often accidents below; a woman was killed three months since by one of the pit waggons. Mother has eight children. Three of us work below; we are her only support'.

Describing the conditions and work of the 'putters' the Sub-Commissioner felt it necessary to include this footnote after one such typical statement made to him:

'It is almost incredible to believe that human beings can submit to such employment, crawling on hands and knees, harnessed like horses, over soft, slushy floors more difficult than dragging the same weights through our lowest common sewers, and more difficult in consequence of the inclination, which is frequently one in three to one in six'.

Alexander Gray was a pump boy, 10 years old. His evidence gives a clear description of the nature of his work:

'I pump out the water in the under-bottom of the pit to keep the men's rooms dry. I am obliged to pump fast or the water would cover me. I had to run away a few weeks ago as the water came up so fast that I could not pump at all, and the men were obliged to gang. The water frequently covers my legs, and those of the men when they sit to pick. I have been two years at the pump. I work every day whether the men work or not. I am paid 10d a day; no holiday, but the Sabbath. I go down at three, sometimes five in the morning, and come up at six or seven at night. I know that I work 12 and 14 hours, as I can tell by the clock. I can read and do a little writing'.

Samuel Scriven reported on conditions in the West Riding of Yorkshire. His Report also included an outright condemnation of the use of young girls in the mines. Before looking at some of his findings it is useful perhaps, to include here his own personal reaction, having seen the conditions for himself. His statement has a great deal in common with those of Richard Oastler describing the lot of the factory children. There is an unmistakable passion and outrage in both men, comparing the concern for others overseas with the neglect shown towards young people at home:

'Shall it be said that in the very heart of our own country – from which missions are daily sent to teach God's law, and millions upon millions have been generously poured forth for the manumission of hosts is a distant land – that there shall exist a state of society in which hundreds of young girls are sacrificed to such shameless indecencies, filthy abominations and cruel slavery as is found to exist in our coal pits? Chained, belted, harnessed like dogs in a go-cart, saturated with wet and more than half-naked, crawling upon their hands and feet, and dragging their heavy loads behind them they present an appearance indescribably disgusting and unnatural'.

One of the most famous illustrations from the 'Report on the Employment of Children in Mines' was that of two children, Ann Ambler and William Dyson, being lowered down a shaft together on primitive winding gear. This situation, illustrated from the Yorkshire coalfield, was considered to be morally offensive and extremely primitive in its operation. A young half-naked girl in such close proximity to a boy brought about a strong reaction. Many of the girls told the Commission that they worked naked to the waist, and that the men around them were often entirely naked. John Thornley, Justice of the Peace said of the circumstances:

'Sexual intercourse decidedly frequently occurs in consequence. Cases of bastardy frequently occur, and I am of the opinion that women brought up in this way lay aside all modesty.'

William Dyson and Ann Ambler were both 'hurriers', that is, they pulled the loaded waggons in the same way as the 'putters' described in the Scottish mines. The boy, aged 14, described the girl's circumstances underground, pointing out that she was the only girl employed in that particular mine. She was believed to be 13 years old, and had been 'hurrying' since she was seven years old. Her father worked in another mine nearby:

'She goes down with us upon the clutch harness, she wears her breeches when she goes down and while at work, and comes up the pit cross-lapped with us in the clutch harness. When she is down she hurries with us in the same way as we do, without shoes or stockings. I have seen her thrashed many times when she does not please them, they rap her in the face and knock her down. She does not like her work, I have seen her cry many times; the men swear at her often; she says she will be killed before she leaves the coal pit.'

Margaret Comeley, aged nine, also spoke of being flogged in the pit and that she suffered from bellyache and headache. She told of how she often had a piece of muffin to eat at midday, but pointed out that no time was allowed her to

One of the most effective and startling of the illustrations accompanying the Royal Commission into the coal mines, 1842. It shows two young 'hurriers' (those who moved the coal in wagons etc., from the coal-face itself to the main galleries or shafts), Ann Ambler and William Dyson being drawn up a shaft by a woman operating crude and dangerous winding gear. The colliery employing them was that of Messrs. Ditchforth and Clay at Elland in South Yorkshire. The girl is naked to the waist, and their circumstances were said to have caused considerable comment in Parliament.

stop and eat. It was necessary for her to eat whilst pushing the loaded coal waggons. Again in a footnote, this Sub-Commissioner recorded his personal view, saying that nothing he had seen in the misery of the worst factories was equal to the degredation and suffering witnessed in the mines.

Despite the dangers, moral and physical, many parents were anxious to get their children into the mines in order to help out financially. According to one mother it was extremely difficult to find alternative work for their children and economic hardship dictated that they should seek employment underground:

'I have two girls in the pit; the youngest is 8 and the oldest will be 19 in May. If the girl's don't go into the pits they must take a poke and go begging. I have tried for the oldest to get her place, but not for the others. It is difficult to get them out at first to service. I don't think it makes very much difference, if they have example showed to them, whether they go into the pits or not.'

Another mother responded on similar lines:

'I went to the pit myself when I was five years old, and two of my daughters go now. It does them no harm. It never did me none. My girls learn to sew as much as I can teach them, but thats not much. One sews well. They have told me that all the children are to be taken out of the pits, and I don't know what we shall do.'

At this point the Sub-Commissioner reported that the witness broke down, and he explained that she was 'overpowered with fear' at the prospect that the children might be removed from the mines.

Looking briefly at the evidence from South Durham, the mining community therewas seen to be equally as anxious that children should work on a permanent basis. An official of the South Hetton colliery stated that they were constantly beset by parents concerned that their young children should be employed. Many of these children were described as being less than nine years old.

Conditions in the Lancashire coalfield, an extensive employer of female labour, revealed further examples of considerable hardship. Betty Harris aged 37, and a drawer (hauling loaded coal waggons) offered a powerful and vivid picture of her life in the mines at that time. Her evidence, based on employment at Little Bolton, Lancashire, stands in complete contrast with those interests inside and outside the industry who argued that work below ground was not harmful:

'I was married at 33 and went into the colliery when I was married. I used to weave when about 12 years old, and can neither read nor write. I work at Andrew Knowles of Little Bolton and make sometimes seven shillings a week, sometimes not so much. I am a drawer and work from six o'clock in the morning to six at night. Stop about an hour to eat my dinner; have bread and butter for dinner; I get no drink. I have two children but they are too young to work. I worked at drawing when I was in the family way. I know of a woman who has gone home and washed herself, taken to her bed, been delivered of a child, and gone to work under a week.

I have a belt round my waist, and a chain passing between my legs, and I go on my hands and feet. The road is very steep, and we have to hold by a rope; and when there is no rope by anything we can catch hold of. There are about six women and about six boys and girls in the pit I work in; it is very hard work for a woman. The pit is very wet where I work, and the water comes over our clog tops always, and I have seen it up to my thighs; it rains in at the roof terribly; my clothes are wet through almost all day long. I never was ill in my life, but when I was lying in. My cousin looks after my children in the day time; I am very tired when I get home at night. I fall asleep sometimes before I get washed. I am not so strong as I was, and cannot stand my work as well as I used to. I have drawn till I have had the skin off me; the belt and chain is worse when we are in the family way. My feller (husband) has beaten me many a time for not being ready. I were not used to it at first and he had little patience. I know many a man beat his drawer. I have known men take liberty with the drawers, and some of the women have bastards.'

Further illustration of 'hurrying' or putting at it was known in Scotland. The loading of the wagons or carts varied from between 3 and 9 or 10 cwt.

No.	Date.	Where.	Name.	Age.	Verdicts.
	1837				
1	Dec. 26 .	Saddleworth .	Mills, Richard	..	Fell from a corve in ascending the shaft of a coal-pit. Deceased and another boy in the corve with a collier, and was properly cautioned.
	1838				
2	Jan. 2 .	Bierley . .	Thorp, Joseph	52	A banksman, fell down the shaft, in landing the corve had neglected to slip the catch.
3	Feb. 1 .	Lindley . .	Walker, George	26	Fall of a stone from the shaft side. No neglect.
4	March 7 .	Bowling . .	Root, Edward	13	Fell from the corve in descending. Supposed to have caught at something on the pit's side.
5	March 22	Holmfirth .	Hurst, Enoch .	10	Killed by a piece of coal falling from the corve. No blame; he might have got out of the way.
6	April 28.	North Bierley	Sugden, Abraham	9	Fall of ironstone from a corve. No blame or negligence.
7	May 2 .	Bradford Moor	Walker, William .	16	Thrown from a corve to the bottom of the shaft by the rope breaking—the engineer neglecting to stop his rope in proper time; the boy coming up without notice, and contrary to the rules.
8	June 22 .	Wilsden . .	Binns, Abraham .	15	Fall of scale from a corve hitting against the ledges of the shaft.
9	July 5 .	Northowram .	Crossley, John .	16	Ditto ditto, in consequence of wet weather.
10	July 10 .	Ditto . . .	Crossley, Abraham	30	The like.
11	Aug. 3 .	North Bierley	Anson, Christopher	7	Accidental fall down a shaft; a "gin" driver. No blame.
12	Aug. 31 .	Halifax . .	Taylor, Francis .	11	Explosion of fire-damp. Neglect of John Crossley, his master, in not going first in pit.
13	April 17	Ditto . . .	Lumley, James .	9	The like. With caution there is no need of safety-lamps in this district.
14	April 22	Baildon . .	Craven, Joseph .	7	Accidental fall in going down a shaft.
15	Oct. 9 .	Northowram.	Oldfield, Thomas .	48	The like, in consequence of machinery being out of gear. No blame.
	1839				
16	March 1 .	Southowram .	Gray, Joseph . .	11	Accidental fall of a stone from the roof of a pit.
17	March 25	Idle . . .	Hardaker, John .	8	Accidental fall down a shaft. Deceased a cart-driver.
18	April 19 .	Allerton . .	Stansfield, Joshua	8	The like. Deceased not very sharp.
19	April 26.	Tong . . .	Oates, Henry . .	..	Accidental fall down an old shaft. Afterwards filled up at request of jury.
20	May 11 .	Bowling . .	Tewdale, James .	9	Fall from a corve in ascending a shaft.
21	Aug. 13 .	Kirkheaton .	Drake, William .	12	Deceased trying to ascend the shaft by taking hold the axles of the corve, and letting go within a few yards of the top.
22	Sept. 3 ,	Holmfirth .	Barraclough, Joseph	14	Unexpected explosion of fire-damp.
23	Oct. 4 .	North Bierley	West, Joshua . .	9	Fall from a corve in ascending a shaft contrary to rules.
24	Oct. 14 .	Northowram .	Jennings, James .	11	Accidental fall down a shaft by attempting to ascend by tackling without corve.
25	Nov. 19 .	Wilsden . .	Fetley, Benjamin .	14	Ditto ditto of earth from the roof of a pit by deceased driving corve against a post.
26	Dec. 6 .	Bradford . .	Brook, Joseph . .	13	Ditto ditto of stone from the roof of pit.
	1840				
27	March 2 .	Bowling . .	Naylor, James . .	..	Fall of dirt from a corve. The corve not properly fastened by deceased.
28	April 6 .	Wyke . .	Marsden, William	42	Explosion of fire-damp, caused by deceased taking the top from his lamp.
29	April 11.	Bowling . .	Beaumont, Benj. .	..	Killed by coal-waggons. Cautioned to keep out of the way.
30	April 28.	Lindley . .	Wilkinson, William	21	Accidental fall of earth from roof of pit.
31	May 18 .	Southowram .	Cheatham, Charles	10	Explosion of fire-damp, Isaac Green, his employer, neglecting to fill up an old hole.
32	June 1 .	Thornton .	Fearnsides, Thomas	20	Accidental fall from corve in descending the shaft.
33	June 11 .	Halifax . .	Sheard, William .	30	Explosion of fire-damp, deceased persisting in going into the pit, although warned at seeing the fire-damp as he went on.
34	June 15 .	Ditto . . .	Sheard, Joseph .	..	Explosion of fire-damp. Deceased compelled to go in by Wm. Sheard, his employer.
35	Aug. 15 .	Bradley . .	Haigh, Reuben .	12	Accidentally caught in a chain of a corve, and falling whilst drawing up.
36	Aug. 14 .	North Bierley	Sharp, Joseph .	33	Unexpected fall of coal from the roof of a pit.
37	Aug. 22 .	Lockwood .	Haigh, David . .	..	Accidental explosion of fire-damp. Deceased aware of it, and fetching his tools contrary to order.
38	,,	Ditto . . .	Jephson, Joshua .	..	The like.
39	Sept. 15 .	Horton . .	Fieldhouse, Thomas	5	Accidental fall down a shaft, deceased playing near the pit in the absence of the workpeople.
40	Sept. 23 .	North Bierley	Worship, Noah .	11	Killed in pit by a corve running over him, deceased going before instead of behind the corve.
41	Nov. 2 .	Northowram .	Woodhead, John .	29	Accidental fall from a corve in ascending the shaft.
42	Nov. 17 .	North Bierley	Smith, James . .	13	Killed in pit by a corve falling on him.
43	Dec. 18 .	Ditto . . .	Brook, Jonas . .	38	Unexpected fall of earth from the roof of pit.
44	,,	Wike . . .	Heaton, John . .	20	The like.
	1841				
45	Jan. 21 .	Tong . . .	Thomas, Benjamin	12	Explosion of gunpowder, deceased intending to secrete a portion.
46	,,	Bowling . .	Hill, John . . .	..	Accidental fall down a shaft in landing a corve.
47	Jan. 22 .	Ditto . .	Sharp, Joseph .	12	Ditto ditto ditto.
48	Feb. 26 .	Halifax . .	Sutcliffe, Jonathan	..	Accidental and unexpected explosion of fire-damp.
49	April 10 .	Northowram .	Smith, Mathew .	..	Fall down a shaft, deceased holding the clatch-irons without giving notice to draw up.
50	June 12 .	North Bierley	Kellett, David .	14	Fall down a shaft. Deceased drawn over the pulley by his uncle and grand-father.

Returns on deaths from accidents and explosions in the Bradford and Halifax District, December 1838 – June 1841.

Trapping, the task of opening and closing the ventilation doors when the coal waggons passed by, was work given to the very youngest children in the mine. The doors controlled the flow of air through the workings and helped to prevent the build-up of pockets of gas. Trappers of six years and in one case, five years old were noted in Northumberland and Durham coalfields.

The evidence of John Otterson a 13 year old on the South Durham coalfield offers a useful description of the young trapper:

'I became a door-keeper on the barrow-way four years ago. I got up at four o'clock took breakfast and walked to the pit by half past four; began work at five. I had no candles allowed at all, except my father gave me any, he gave me four which burned about five hours, and I sat in darkness the rest of the time. I liked it very badly, it was like as if I was transported. I used to sleep: I could not keep my eyes open. The overman used to bray (hit) us with the yard wand; he used to leave the marks; I used to be afraid. The 'putters' sometimes thumped me for being asleep. They never gave me any money. We loose at five and come home. I got my dinner, washed; I took off all my clothes, and went to bed about eight. I did not go to play, the more we play the more we sleep in the pit.'

Here also is the statement of Sarah Gooder, aged eight, and a trapper at Gauber Pit in the West Riding of Yorkshire:

'I am a trapper in the Gauber Pit. I have to trap without a light and I am scared. I go at four and sometimes half past three in the morning, and come out at five and half-past. I never go to sleep.

Sometimes I sing when I've light, but not in the dark; I dare not sing then. I don't like being in the pit.'

This simple, factual statement serves as a clear indication of the circumstances of such children. Eloquent in its simplicity, it emphasises solitude, darkness and fear which they endured for long hours each working day.

Many trappers played games in the darkness and solitude, a favourite being to catch mice, beetles and midges. The Commissioner reporting on Lancashire considered trapping to be an activity 'equal to solitary confinement of the worst order; one of the most pitiable occupations in the coal-pit'. From returns on the Northumberland and Durham coalfield the largest number of trappers were between the ages of 8 and 11 years; 9 to 10 years of age being the category with the highest number.

Mining communities were often isolated and insular. They could also vary in what the Commissioners called their moral and physical condition. Drunkenness was a common vice widely reported, likewise large numbers of miners and their families were said to ignore religion and attendance at church or chapel. Not only were the communities isolated, they were often quite new. A large

Three views of 'putting' in the Lothian in the Lothian coalfield. According to the description given by the Royal Commission: "Putters drag or push the carts containing coal, from the coal-wall to the pit-bottom, weight varying from three to ten cwt."

population could move into a previously unpopulated area when mining began making a community devoid of many or all of the institutions which had long characterised village or town life. The Methodists for their part were the most energetic in establishing contact within mining areas. They opened chapels and schools in many areas far removed from the influence of the Church of England, their concern being noted especially in the North East, parts of Lancashire and Yorkshire, and amongst the tin and copper mining districts of Cornwall, for example.

Actual communities varied, both large and small. Where the coalowner showed an active interest in the community the general moral and physical conditions could be very favourable. This was certainly so in West Scotland where a Mr Macready of Pearson, near Irvine in Ayrshire opened a new pit and provided something of a model community for the workforce. The housing was described as follows:

'The house consists of a kitchen 18 feet 6 inches by 12 feet, having a bed-place on the side opposite the fire, a press or closet between this and the door, and one window. Out of the kitchen open two doors into small bedrooms, nine feet by six, having each a window. The separate rooms afford accommodation for lodgers, and also the means of washing and dressing apart from the family. The floors are made of a kind of concrete, of lime and gravel. In the centre of the row of 15 of these cottages is a higher building designed for the school room. The houses also had gardens and good privies.'

Similar improvements in the Kilmarnock district by other managers and coalowners led to great advancement in children's education with limitations imposed on working

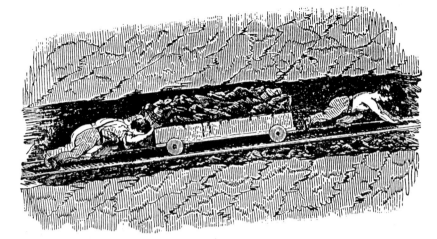

Three young children hurrying or drawing a loaded waggon of coals. The child in front is harnessed by his belt or chain to the waggon; the two boys behind are assisting in pushing it forward.

Scenes such as this of Margaret Hills employed in the Scottish Lothian Coalfield, and, indeed, all such employment, caused the commissioners to denounce the work as no more than "base feudalism", and "a disgrace to the Christian country."

hours and at the age which young people entered the mines. The active presence of the surgeon and minister made for improvements whilst a library and a school emphasised the value of education. The Gatehead Colliery described here and managed by Mr John Muir became a model of its kind. Children were not permitted to enter the mine unless they were at least ten years of age and held a certificate indicating an adequate level of education. The truck system was also banned at these mines whereas the pernicious device was commonplace across the mining communities of West Scotland. Good sturdy housing with gardens was also provided.

Below ground, trap doors were operated by adults, and when young people began their employment they were given shorter hours than others in order to get used to the process gradually.

The Commissioners' returns on Northumberland and North Durham included several references to the fact that in many pit villages miners enjoyed a good standard of living. Their material comforts were considerable when compared, for instance, with the lot of many agricultural labourers in the South of England. Substantially built houses with ample heating and ventilation were noted, together with the fact they were largely well furnished:

'These houses, generally congregated together, and arranged in the manner of streets or squares; a small plot of land to grow potatoes is being allotted to each house. The pigsty is in front, where are also deposited the ashes, off scouring and coals. A pit cottage consists of two rooms with a pantry, therooms are paved with bricks, and above it, an open attic unceiled.'

It was also said that the communities generally ate heartily. According to William Morrison, of Chester-le-Street, medical gentleman engaged at the Countess of Durham's collieries:

'The children of colliers are comfortably and decently clothed; cleanliness, both in their persons and houses, is a predominant feature in the domestic economy of the female part of the community. Pitmen, of all labouring classes I am acquainted with, enjoy most the pleasure of good living; their larders abound in potatoes, bacon, fresh meat, sugar, tea and coffee, of which good things the children as abundantly partake as the parents; even the sucking infant, to its prejudice is loaded with as much of the greasy and well seasoned riands of the table as it will swallow. In this respect the women are foolishly indulgent, and I know of no class of persons among whom infantile diseases so much prevail.'

At Walker Colliery, Newcastle, the Mine Surgeon, Mr. Greenhow, described the dwellings as 'generally pretty well constructed and well warmed'. Whilst the population was said to be clean and well clothed, for the most part, the correspondent did state that there were 'great distinctions in neatness, cleanliness, order and general comfort' depending upon the inclination of the specific household. Methodism was said to 'prevail largely in the collieries' and the local community at Walker was described as teetotal. A representative of the Monkwearmouth Colliery informed the commission that 'the Methodists have a great hold on the pit people, and although I am not of that persuasion I must say that Methodists have done more to ameliorate the pitmen than the whole Church put together'. Also included in the report was the inevitable reference to drink and to its effects; 'Drunkenness is prevalent here'. It was argued that proximity to the town of Sunderland had a detrimental effect upon the colliery people – 'fairs, dances, theatres, etc., seduce them'. The lack of interest in education, for themselves and for their children was considered one of the most serious criticisms of the mining population

Three illustrations of girls' dress in the Scottish mines of Fifeshire and Mid Lothian.

and this, together with their apparent concern for a variety of pleasures and destractions on Sundays, appeared to stand as a general observation for almost all the major colliery districts. William Hunter, agent for Backworth Colliery (Northumberland and North Durham) provided the following statement on education in his district:

'Amongst the pitboys my opinion is that education is both deficient in quantity and quality; this arises chiefly from the following causes, namely the apathy of the parents to education, and to the boys being sent down the pits so early, say at the of 7 or 8; the unfitness of many of the schoolmasters, and the great want of punctuality of parents in paying for the tuition of their children.'

The agent's views on education found widespread support from other contributions to the Report. He called for full time education to the age of 11, but could not see real progress without actual Government intervention.

The mining community of Wigan was described in a decidedly unfavourable light by the Relieving Officer for the district in 1841. In contrast to the references given elsewhere detailing reasonable material conditions, the housing at Wigan was described as follows:

'The houses are usually filthy; there is no attention to whitewashing or ventilation; paper and rags are often paste and stuffed into broken windows; the beds and bedding are generally poor; In many parts of the town, indeed, in all excepting the principal streets, the drainage is entirely neglected; ditches containing filth and putrefying matter, and lodgements of standing water, make the atmosphere in the neighbourhood of the town. There are many rows of houses with only a single privy to them all. There have been constant fevers for the last two or three winters in some parts of the town, and I have no doubt that the filth of the streets and houses have mainly been the cause of it.'

Turning to the general moral condition of the population, the correspondent offered an equally bleak report:

'Generally speaking they are a class of people ignorant and illiterate, and they are scarcely ever in the habit of visiting places of worship. The alehouses throng on Saturday nights.'

The Relieving Officer of the Hindley district supported these statements adding that the girls locally, 'had no shame about them and were very bold and course in their language

Women coal-bearer(s) in East Scotland.

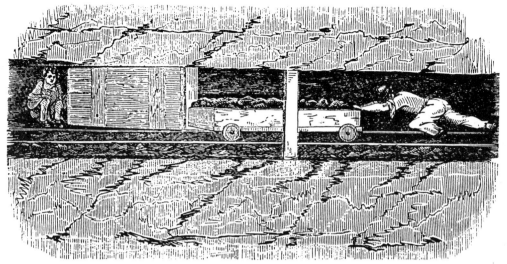

A young trapper at work. Writing on the circumstances of the trappers in Lancashire, the sub-commissioner wrote; "This occupation is one of the most pitiable in a coal-pit from its extreme monotony. Their whole time is spent sitting in the dark for 12 hours – were it not for the passing of wagons it would be equal to solitary confinement of the worst order."

and much given to swearing'! Boys, it was claimed, were 'frequently seen at the public houses with their fathers, smoking, singing and drinking like the rest'.

In many respects the mining community lived on the very edge of civilised society. Exposed, as they surely were, to every conceivable danger below ground and with often no consideration shown them regarding their welfare, even down to young children, both their lifestyle and work marked them out quite distinctively amongst the overall working population. The often harsh and raucous nature of their society must surely have been something of a reflection and expression of their overall situation. The pages of the 1842 Report and, indeed the newspapers of the day, carried ample evidence of the daily hazards confronting miners. The constant danger of sudden death from the explosion of gas deposits, or from flooding or subsidence, together with the more long-term sentence from the insidious effects of physical fatigue, heat, damp and dust made for a hostile and unrelenting environment difficult for us to really appreciate today.

The Mines Act of August 1842 was largely welcomed as a much needed reform. As indicated earlier, however, in certain cases working people themselves opposed the legislation. In banning girls and women from the pits and banning boys below the age of ten, many working families feared extreme financial hardship. Other interests also opposed reform for a number of reasons.

In May 1841 a committee purporting to represent the Yorkshire Coal Owners offered its response to the Commission on Children's Employment. Actual legislation on behalf of children and young people was in the Committee's view, on a par with the existing Factory Act -' a violation of every maxim of civil and commercial freedom'. Opposition to the idea of intervention continued, covering issues of hours, child labour, education and the principle of inspection and intervention, ('espionage'):

'To restrict the hours of working is wholly impossible. The limitation of age, while it would be productive of increased expense in all cases, would oblige the owners of this seem to abandon their mines, which they have opened at great expense. The system of espionage, and the powers of the inspector would in the case of the mines be still more intolerable, from the varied and constantly changing nature of the operation of mining;

the technical difficulties which attend it, and the danger of entrusting any controlling power in the management of the mines on their machinery to persons who would be entirely ignorant of the principles and practice of the art. To attempt to extend a compulsory system of education to children employed in mines would be fruitless on account of the nature of the employment, the distance at which they reside from the pit and the constantly changing position of the pits themselves.'

In the Northumberland and North Durham collieries, the Agent for the Countess of Durham, Henry Morton, made the following points:

'Thinks that the usual employment of the children in coal mines is perfectly consistent with their health. Working a night shift does not make much difference and in any way injure them. Has never heard of any boys straining or rupturing themselves in the pits. Does not think any alterations in the hours of labour necessary for children. There is no prospect of carrying on collieries so as to dispense with the labours of very young children; any restricting law that should produce a scarcity of children would prevent many pits from being carried on beneficially; old men, to supplant trappers, and what are called swing doors, are inapplicable. There is a great want of veracity amongst the boys. and all their statements must be received with the greatest caution. Would depreciate any legislative interference and thinks that would be the general wish of owners.'

Lord Londonderry, together with other coalowners in the House of Lords, opposed the free passage of the 1842 Mines Bill. Their intervention succeeded in removing the important clause relating to reports on the condition of the mines and machinery. The latter was not made law until 1850. Deeply critical of the 1842 legislation, Lord Londonderry attacked what he considered to be the lurid and sensational manner in which the case for reform was developed, in particular the use of actual illustrations below ground. His opposition was that he attempted (in 1843) an Act to repeal the measures gained during the previous year. Such opposition, however, could at best only delay further reform.

A 'gigger', or boy who controls the brake on simple winding machinery in the inclined shaft. Boys, as seen here in the Manchester area, of only 10 years were put in charge of such duties. Following the 1842 Mines Act, all boys below the age of 16 were barred from operating winding machinery.

A recurring statement in the pages of the 1842 Report was that relating to the difficulty faced by girls in search of employment outside the coal industry. Very few girls, it was said, were suitable to become household servants on account of the negative influence of their pit background. Their situation was made increasingly difficult when, from 1 March 1843, they were barred from work underground. The Walkden Moor Servants' School, near Worsley, Manchester founded in 1843 was intended to provide training to enable girls to become housemaids, laundrymaids, and kitchen assistants. Accommodation was available for 12 girls and included board, lodging, clothing and tuition. Part of the day was spent in lessons at the adjoining girls' school and thereafter, household duties and work in the garden were followed. The girls at the school were aged from 14 to 20 and their course was of 12 months duration.

Included in the Appendix at the back of this book are the official rules and regulations of the establishment underlining the strict discipline imposed upon the girls, in view of their particular background.

The Report on the Operation of the Act 5 and 6 Vict, and on the State of the Mining Population, 1844, gave detailed consideration to the problems confronting women and girls no longer able to work in the mines. Deprived of their livlihood, many women found life very difficult, particularly when there was no family to offer financial support.

A return from the parish of Newton in Mid Lothian explained the situation. The Act was said to have 'materially affected the well-being of the families, however beneficial it may be in the end, and, especially, has proved a sore grievance to females somewhat advanced in life who have no rear relatives to support them'. The actual number of females affected was 180. 61 were married and returned to the home and their children; of the remaining 119 only 49 obtained regular employment, 10 in factories, the rest as domestic servants. The remainder, being 70, also included the young people from nine years of age upward. Many of this remaining group, including the more elderly, never again found active employment, whilst the Poor Law regulations added to their plight. Being fit and, therefore, able to work, should it be available, they were not even entitled to parish assistance.

Whilst efforts were made by certain coalowners to provide alternative employment for women, many left their former employees to their own resources. At Wigan and Chorley some colliery owners continued to employ females in defiance of the 1842 Act. The Report on the Mining Population, 1847 took a dim view of such activities. Referring to the district as being 'behind other communities in civilised ideas and habits', the Report stated:

'It is unfortunate that this district should be amongst the very few still to be found in the kingdom in which there are coal proprietors who are not unwilling to connive at the employment of females in their collieries. The injustice of this course of conduct to neighbouring proprietors, who put themselves to so much trouble, and deny themselves advantages, in order to faithfully observe the law, is the subject of well-founded complaint.'

Complaint was also made by coal-owners in the West Riding of Yorkshire and in several Scottish coal fields with regard to neglect or indifference to children's education by the miners themselves. A representative of the Bierly collieries in the Bradford district made the following statement with reference to this issue:

'We have no boys at work under 10. Plenty of the colliers' boys under 10 attend no day school; only a few do. The reason is that the parents are not wishful for the education of their children. Not many of the boys can read when they come to us first to work.'

A superintendent at the Bowley Iron Works again, near Bradford also commented on the lack of interest in education by the workforce:

'We have above 500 men and 200 boys in and about our pit. The boys under 10, who are prevented by the Act from going down the pit, do not go to school; it is very rare that they do; they remain idling about; or if their parents can get them into a mill, or do any odd job, they do so. They (the colliers) send their boys to the mills and live upon them if they choose to be idle themselves.'

By 1847 the Report on Operation of 1842 Act/State of Mining Population offered a somewhat bleak view of the future if the 1842 Act was not linked to basic measures in education.

'In regard to the boys, as the Act of Parliament forbids their being employed below ground until they are 10 years old ... it is highly desirable that some portion at least of the years rescued from the labour of the mine, should be devoted, according to the benevolent intention of the legislature, to opening the faculties and training the dispositions of these children by means of day school. At present nearly a whole generation of these boys is growing up as undisciplined and ignorant as the majority of the present race of adults.'

Fearful for the future with large numbers of ill disciplined uneducated people comprising the workforce, the Report painted a picture of what it called 'a sensual, ignorant and demoralised people, rude and repulsive'.

In Scotland there was considerable support for a scheme whereby boys would be required to produce a certificate of education for their employer before being allowed to commence work. This, it was hoped, would bring the mines more into line with factory legislation, emphasising the active provision of education. Progress followed, slowly but surely.

The Mines Act of 1860 emphasised the importance of education and took a furtive step when it increased the minimum age for children working below ground to 12 years, or 10 years of age where a relevant certificate was produced. Children were increasingly being directed away from the mines and, indeed, many other forms of employment as the need for education became more widely recognised.

The adult miners at the coal face. As shown here, they worked naked or semi-naked according to custom.

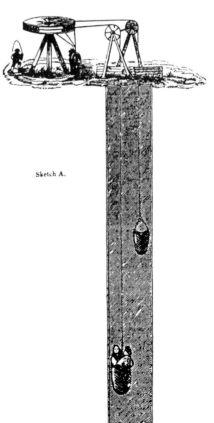

Sketch A.

Chapter Four
The Tin and Copper Mines

Cornwall and parts of West Devon were rich in copper and tin during the last century. Both these minerals were worked extensively with the result that in many mines the principal advednturers and share-holders became rich from their investments. Entire communities developed around groups of mines, or, in some cases, around a single mine, and were sustained by the wealth from underground. Tin and copper mining, especially the latter, supported a very large population and became the mainspring of the local economy for much of the century. Rural parishes such as Gwennap had a population of over 10,000 in the 1840s, larger than that of the main towns, other than Truro.

Men, women and children were employed in mining, but in tin and copper production, women and girls did not work underground. Nor, indeed, were young boys employed to any extent below ground. This made for the important difference between metaliferrous mines of the far west and the collieries in certain other parts of Britain, the latter, employing both women and young children below ground until 1842.

The Mining Journal of January 1858 offered a detailed account of the (surface) work of young people in the mining industry, emphasising the employment of the 'bal-maidens'; 'bal' meaning mine. In many respects George Henwood's account stresses several similar or related themes to those raised elsewhere in industry or agriculture. The moral dimension is a particular case in point as, indeed, it appeared to take precedence over the physical nature of the work and the accompanying hardship. When compared, for example, with the material on the Gang System of Eastern England the criticisms and priorities have a lot in common. Compare also the observations and judgements on matter of dress and general behaviour with those addressed to the girls in the lace industry of East Devon.

'On many mines, particularly in the tin mines, large numbers of boys and girls are employed in dressing the ores in many of the larger mines scores of 'bal-maidens', as they are termed are employed in and in certain parts of the work almost as equal number of boys. Whilst at their work and under the supervision of the master dresser all goes tolerably well, save course joking and that continued association we must complain of; at meal time and going to and from their work it is almost impossible to prevent that conversation and rude behaviour we so much wish to see prevented.

On some of the larger and better regulated mines there are separate and comfortable dining rooms provided for each sex, where decency and order are strictly observed. This is a step in the right direction and a great improvement. The evil is known to and admitted by all mining agents who respect the necessity, but can see no remedy for it. The same supineness formerly existed with respect to females employed in the collieries; the agents could not see how the evil was to be avoided until the public saw for themselves and compelled them to adopt an improved regime.

The maidens are usually sent to the mines at an age of 6 to 7 years, where they are taught to assort the ores, after which they learn to 'buck' and jig them – that is bruise and separate by water the ores of copper, lead and zinc; a most laborious species of work, particularly the bruising of the ore which is done by striking the pieces with a heavy hammer on a flat piece of iron. In larger ore producing mines, huge crushers or rollers are employed; in the smaller, the bal-maidens have this to do, but if actively pursued is too hard work for females.

In tin mines these girls attend to the frames which is comparatively light and clean work, but continual exposure to wet is unfit for females, whilst the constant association with the men and boys is highly improper. These poor girls remain from the early age mentioned until they either get married off to some of the miners or die of consumption, which carries off hundreds annually.

The hard work is not the greatest calamity of which we complain, that is a mere physical evil. What we most deplore is that when called to take upon themselves the duties of wife and mother they are entirely unfit for them. How can the moral standards of society amongst the lower orders be raised by mothers and sisters with such education and example? It is utterly hopeless. Taken from their hearth at such an early age and kept at work for ten hours a day, they have little opportunity and less inclination to attend to the matronly duties so necessary for their future and well being. Their being associated in such numbers and before men, a spirit of rivalry in dress is soon engendered and every attention – all their thoughts and earnings – are devoted to the methods of making themselves attractive.

To see the bal-maidens on a Sunday when fully dressed would astonish a stranger; whilst at their work the pendant earrings and showy bead necklaces excite the pity, as well as the surprise of the thoughtful. All desire to save a few shillings for later life is discarded and nothing but display is thought of.

Machinery is rapidly effecting a change and we hail every improvement in that department as a real blessing to miners; but where it dispenses with female labour, in such situation, we rejoice in it as a grand and effective effort towards the domestic comfort of thousands, and as a help towards the elevation of the social position of mankind generally.

If the employment of girls in coal mines is improper, why is such work not improper in mineral mines? We know and feel we shall encounter a host of opponents, rich and poor, to any government interference; that the cry will be: 'Vested rights; you will stop the mines'.'

Looking to Man's basic decency and goodness, the writer concluded his account with a reference to the Almighty:

'We trust in Him, whose ways are not as our ways and abide His time with confidence.'

The strong moral influence is clear here and was of particular concern to the writer. His reference to the fact that, for him, 'hard work is not the greatest calamity of which we complain', serves to illustrate his priority. Whilst acknowledging the harsh physical circumstances of these people's lives he also criticised their particular concern for their appearance in such a way as to seem to suggest that their behaviour was almost sinful. To a certain extent standards varied in different parts of Cornwall, but overall this general picture applied, with many of the points being made earlier in the Royal Commission of 1842. For example, Dr. Barham wrote for the Commission, 'the love of display is shown in the wearing of their shoes and stockings during weather in which they are unsuitable'. Women and girls were apparently spending more on more expensive outer garments for 'personal attraction' than they were for warmer and more practical inner garments. 'A passion for dress' was the expression used by Dr. Barham in describing the physical appearance of the bal-maidens.

Groups of bal-maidens employed at the surface works of a Cornish copper mine in the mid nineteenth century. Said to have a weakness for 'showy' clothes and over-dressing generally, many of these girls died from consumption by their thirties as a result of exposed working conditions, the labour itself, their general poor health, and their environment.

In the Report of the 'Royal Commission on the Environment of Children', evidence submitted in 1842, Dr. Charles Barham stated that the number of children and young people employed in the mines of West Devon and Cornwall was between 9,000 and 10,000. Of these approximately 3,000 were under 13 years of age, whilst amongst the young people above 13 years the greater proportion was female.

From evidence given to the Commission boys began work at the surface between 8 and 9 years of age, and the girls between 9 and 10. In certain cases children were brought to work at earlier ages as a result of Poor Law regulations. Mothers complained to mining agents that under workhouse rules 'they could not get bread for them (their children) and were thus forced to send them to work.

Employment underground was always the ambition of boys, who gradually began this work from about the age of 12 or 13. According to Dr. Barham 'a few boys go underground between the ages of 9 or 10. The number increases with every year afterwards'. The proportion of boys working underground varied according to factors such as the particular area, the demands of the mines themselves and the availability of labour. Prestige, higher pay and shorter hours of work were the incentives to go underground but this work was extremely exacting, far more so than employment at the surface. The main forms of work for boys below

ground were with ventilation or tramming, (moving waggons of stone or ore).

Two extracts from the Commission of Children's Employment (Mines) will serve to give details of working conditions. The first describes surface employment:

'The usual length of the working day for surface labourers in these mines is ten hours in summer and about nine in winter. Work begins at seven in the morning in summer, and with daylight in winter, and it concludes at five, half-past five, or six, or when it grows dark. Half-an-hour, three quarters, or a whole hour, is allowed for dinner in different districts and in one instance, two hours. A short interval is, in a few cases only, permitted at 10 am. On the other hand, the hours of work are often prolonged until seven or eight in the evening; and in some cases work is begun an hour earlier than usual in the mornings as well.

In these cases the day is sometimes disposed of as follows:

A boy or girl from nine to twelve years old, is obliged to rise at about 4 am, gets a heavy breakfast, and after a walk of an hour or more – three or four miles – reaches the mine at six. Work is continued till twelve, without intermission or refreshment save what may be got by stealth. Half an hour is then employed in taking dinner. The child then works without interruption till eight; gets home, after repeating the walk of the morning and may have had supper, and gets to bed about ten. It is chiefly the younger children who are called upon to begin their work at 6 am, the process on which they are engaged being preparatory for the other.'

The second exact deals with work underground.

'The most frequent arrangement of time with underground work is the division of the twenty four hours into three 'courses' of eight hours each with three relays, so that the place of work is never unoccupied. In this case the relays usually succeed each other at 6 am, 2 pm and 10 pm. Whatever arrangement is adopted by the miners, the boys are included in it, and continue at work during the same time, except that six hours of the harder work of wheeling barrows is sometimes equivalent to eight hours lighter work and they are then allowed to go up before the men, if the stuff

Botallack Mine near St Just, West Cornwall. This famous mine, visited by royalty and celebrated for its magnificent cliff-side setting, employed some 300 men, 116 females and 115 boys in the mid 1860s. Tin and copper were both mined here beneath the sea.

that they have been employed in removing has been cleared away. The night work is taken by the boys equally with the men where boys are employed at all by the party.'

Together with those in working communities across Britain, the young people of the copper mining districts suffered with regard to education. The rich copper producing area of West Devon, between Tavistock and the River Tamar, was no exception as this statement on Gulworthy School in Tavistock parish reveals. The source here is the Report on Children, Young People and Women in Agriculture in 1867:

'This school is in the centre of a mining district, mixed and 130 on the books – The children are about 20 per cent agricultural, a larger number, miners, and a very few farmer's sons. The attendance begins to decrease at about 11 years old; mostly they go to mining work, but a few as farm labourers. They are employed in the mines as young as nine years, above ground, for dressing ore. The school draws from a population of quite 2000, still there are a great many children in this district who never get any schooling at all, their parents are careless about it, but few are too poor to pay the one penny a week.'

Dr. Barham's report on children and young people linked with the copper and tin mines (1842) included certain recommendations for improvements. To provide a more positive working environment the following proposals were considered appropriate:

1. No child should be employed in any way in a mine under nine years of age.
2. No boy should be employed underground before 15 years of age.
3. No child on surface work should be employed for more than eight out of twenty-four hours, until they were 13, and ten hours, until they are 18.
4. Night work should not be permitted under the age of 15.
5. Not less than ¾ hour should be allowed for dinner.
6. The substitution of manual labour in several cases, and more appropriate work in view of age and strength.
7. No employment of boys under 15 years of age on engines (machinery).
8. Education for children and young persons.

With one exception, little, however, was done on their behalf prior to the introduction of full-time, compulsory education as all the evidence here, after 1842, illustrates. The Mines Act of 1872 extended the improved conditions of those in the coal mines to others working in metalliferous mines. Barham's recommendations of 1842 found support by this later date as legislation from 1872 now covered children's employment and matters of safety and inspection.

Chapter Five

Brickmaking

The brickfields of Bridgwater in Somerset, provided the main means of employment in the town and surrounding district during the mid 19th century. It was estimated that some four to six thousand people, men, women and children, relied upon the industry for their livelihood. Children made up a considerable section of the work force, being employed mainly as 'Up-strikers – those carrying lumps of clay to the moulder, barrow loaders (Off strikers) and wheel barrowers, Off-bearers.

Brickmaking was outdoor work normally carried on during the months of April to September with some further extension of the season at a lesser pace in March and October. During the winter no bricks were made, but clay was dug for the next season by men and older boys. Whilst hours each day varied from one yard to another, a typical day's work was that from 6 am to 7 pm. Being outdoor work, brick making was dependent upon the weather; wet days saw no work at all.

John Long, a brick-moulder at the Saltland Works, Bridgwater, described the work:

Two boys and two girls work for me. The two boys are half up-strikers and bring me the lumps of clay. One of them is my son, and is now about 10. Next year he will be fit to be a 'whole up-striker' ie. do all that work himself without another boy. Boys are suitable for this work from 9 years old. The little girl (aged 9 and in her second summer of employment) takes the bricks from me when I have moulded them, and places them on a barrow close by, and is called a 'barrow loader'. The big girl is a 'bearer off' and wheels away the bricks and places them in the row or 'back' out in the yard to dry. She gets 2s. 3d. a day, and out of that she has to pay the little girl 4d. The little girl has to turn out at about 5 in the morning to come to work and doesn't leave here until about 7 pm. That is long hours for 4d. Her work looks easy but there is a deal of work attached to it besides loading the barrow. She has to fetch me a kettle-full of water about eight times a day, to wash up all these boards twice a day, and shovel up sand. The bearer off has to wheel each barrow load of 20 bricks on the average, say, about 50 yards each time, and the same back with the empty barrow, backwards and forwards all day long. For any of these parts of work we have boys or girls, just as it happens. Sometimes you can't get boys and then must be girls. I began barrow loading at just about 7 years old. Plenty begin as young as that now, but I suppose none younger. We usually work from about 5.30 am till 6.30 pm stopping half an hour for breakfast and an hour for dinner, not much less, and on Saturdays leave at 1 pm. In a good days work of the usual length I make 3000 bricks. Each brick, when moulded, weighs 9lbs. Each lump, as brought to me by the 'upstrikers', weighs usually more, according as they judge it more or less nearly, say, on the average 10lbs good.'

A similar story was told at other brickworks in Bridgwater. At Coulthurst, Symons and Co's Brick and Tile Works a foreman told the Commission that 31 boys and 6 girls were employed under the age of 18. The youngest boy was 6 years old; the youngest girl, 9 years of age.

George Field, the father of the 6 year old boy referred to here was a brick maker at the works and contributed the following information:

'My boy works for me as a barrow loader, he is two months over 6 years old. He can do this as handy as a bigger one, or better and is worth 2 shillings a week to me. He worked at it a little last year, for a week or two just to get his hand in. Our regular time is to begin at 6 am, or from that until 7 am, and to leave off at 7 pm.'

At Messrs Brown and Co's Manufacturers one of the managing partners expressed his satisfaction with the conduct of the workers and compared them as a class very favourably with those of the manufacturing classes in other parts of Britain. Correct supervision was considered essential. The manager/owner also went on to consider the question of formal protection for his workers via Act of Parliament.

'As to brickwork, I really think that no regulations are needed. The children's work is all healthy, and their amount of work is small; they work for less than half the year, and during even this time it is safe to say that they do not work on the average more than four days a week. To limit them to half time would be no benefit to them and an injury to trade.'

Despite the statement given that their foremen try to keep the younger children out of employment the Commissioner took evidence from several young people – John Stake, aged 6 years a barrow loader who worked from 6 am to 6.30 pm; William Cross aged 6 years 4 months, a barrow loader in his second year of work; Harriet Gulliver, aged 9 years 5 months, a barrow loader for her father, then in her third year at work; Emma Gulliver aged 12 years, an 'upstriker' for her father. The latter witness described her work:

'Roll the clay into lumps by the mill, and carry two at a time to him from there; one on my head, the other in my hands. Have been here four summers altogether.'

Brickmaking allowed a family group to work together, with the efforts of the young children making a useful contribution to the household income. Working as a family was one of the reasons given for the low age of many of the children. The managing partner's warning that a Factory Act would be of little benefit on account of the loss of earnings was a consideration repeated at many levels. The Factory Reformers themselves recognised that the work-force might well suffer from a loss of earnings and this, indeed, was a point made by Robert Peel as Prime Minister when opposing a point of Factory Legislation in 1844.

Long hours of work from April to September prevented children from gaining any sustained education except for those who took advantage of Sunday Schools. A brick manufacturer at Bridgwater recognised this failing, stating that 'the bulk of children who work in the brick and tile factories in and around Bridgwater are not brought up either to read or write'. Long hours also meant inevitable fatigue but other than this the commission considered the work reasonably healthy.

Concern was expressed over the moral condition of children keeping long and regular hours in adult company, and it was emphasised that the work was unbecoming for females. According to an alderman of the town, no female should be employed in the yards until at least 18 years old. In total opposition to employment of young girls, the alderman maintained that, 'after being trained up in that wild field of liberty they will bear no restraint, and seldom will they become servants at all'.

Evidence from brickfields elsewhere reflected even more distressing conditions. The Rev. Boulby, Rector of Oldbury, near Birmingham drew parallels between navvies and the brickyard girls:

'What navvies are amongst men, brickyard girls are amongst women; the same hard physical toil, the same gay clothing on great occasions, the same reckless demeanour.'

The Rev. Body, Curate of Sedgeley and former Curate of Wednesbury, reported:

'Their mental condition is very bad, and the immorality, even to their head knowledge of morality, lower than the nailers. They become coarse and very masculine, poor wives and mothers in every way.'

An ironmaster, also in communication with the above Reverend gentlemen, supported this view of the wretched state of the brickgirls. The Rev. Body was told by the ironmaster that he considered the brick girls moral and mental condition to be unequalled for depravity by any other class in any other civilised country!

Reporting on the brickfields of Middlesex, the Rev Dennett of Cranford wrote at length on the circumstances of the young people at work:

'The boys and girls for the most part are drying or collecting sand on Sundays so that few attend the Sunday School, but finish the day in sauntering and mischief, and in all sorts of games and gambling. It will be obvious how mischievous and demoralising it is to have boys and girls mixing for months with some of the most depraved and degraded characters. The language that they constantly hear, the blasphemy that is frequently poured forth, the utter want of religion and any religious feelings of any kind, and the ridicule often cast upon the mere observance of the Sunday or religious ordinance, without mentioning the filthy, indecent and shameless habits of many among them, is quite sufficient to satisfy the most sceptical of the baneful effects on an ignorant and juvenile mind.'

Attention was also drawn to the accommodation provided by the brick moulder for his gang; this being a familiar practice in the industry. Such a situation was seen and described as 'a fruitful source of demoralisation'.

Once again, the Rev. Dennett drew attention to the arrangements:

'Each 'moulder' is supposed to lodge, board and 'do' for his gang of seven, and, if these are not all his own family, men, boys and girls sleep in his hut; this consists usually of two, sometimes three rooms, and all on the ground with very little ventilation. The bodies off all are greatly exhausted with the profuse perspiration of the day, so that neither health, cleanliness, nor decency can be much, if at all, regarded; and some of the huts are the perfection of untidiness, dirt and dust.'

By the way of final reference to the young people's circumstances, in particular their lack of education, the schoolmaster of the National School at Crayford in Kent, illustrated the disparity in numbers for school attendance in summer and winter periods. Average attendances for the years 1862-1865 were as follows:

WINTER	SUMMER
1862-63 = 72	1862-63 = 60
1863-64 = 80	1863-64 = 64
1864-65 = 85	1864-65 = 68

At Sittingbourne National School the disparity was much greater:

WINTER	SUMMER
1863 = 95	1863 = 57
1864 = 109	1864 = 69
1865 = 123	1865 = 75

The long term benefits of education and the more immediate material demands to earn money at work remained at odds until the establishment of a recognised, compulsory structure of elementary education from the 1870s onward. Thereafter, the child's place was in school, where the leaving age was progressively increased to reach 12 years of age by the end of the century.

A brickfield scene showing a young girl at work. Of this employment, Lord Shaftesbury wrote "In these brickfields, men, women and children, especially poor female children, are brought down to a point of degradation and suffering lower than the beasts of the field."

Chapter Six
The Climbing Boys

The employment of children as chimney sweeps was widespread during the mid nineteenth century despite the existence of legislation against it. As early as 1788 Parliament had made efforts towards protection via 'An Act for the better Regulation of Chimney Sweepers and their Apprentices' the intention being to prohibit the apprenticeship of boys below eight years of age. The Act of 1840, 'An Act for the Regulation of Chimney Sweepers and Chimneys,' gave further cover.

Massive material evidence as to the employment and the suffering of children as sweeps had been presented to the Select Committee of the House of Lords in 1840 resulting in the successful passage of the Act that same year.

Under the Act anyone who knowingly permitted a child or young person under the age of 21 to enter a chimney would be liable for a fine of from £5 to £10 or a prison sentence not exceeding two months for default in payment. No child under 16 years was to be apprenticed and regulations were also included as to the proper construction of chimneys and to the use of sweeping machines.

By the 1860s, however, there were still a considerable number of boys employed in this wretched work. It was well known that for a short period after 1840 the Act

The London sweep as depicted in Henry Mayhew's work on the poor in London. In all likelihood, his appearance generally would have been less robust, and his clothing less substantial.

met with some success. One chimney sweep indicated to the Commissioners that whereas in 1840 there were 22 men and 22 boys employed in Nottingham, none were to be seen within 4 or 5 years. Speaking for 1862 he claimed the number had again rose to 40 men and 27 boys, adding that in Derbyshire the number of climbing boys is greater in proportion than that of Nottinghamshire.

In giving evidence to the Children's Employment Commissioners in October and November 1862, Mr. George Ruff, Master Sweep, of Upper Parliament Street, Nottingham, included the following:

'The use of boys is much encouraged by the fact that many householders will have their chimneys swept by boys instead of machines. I have myself lost a great amount of custom which I should otherwise have, and some of which I formerly had at large houses and public establishments, because I will not use boys. The reason was not given, but I was not employed after I had refused. I have been sent away even from magistrates' houses, and in some cases even by ladies who have preferred to pity the boys, for refusing to use them.' George Ruff then continued by saying that to a limited extent he employed one of his own children to sweep the most difficult chimneys, but soon after stopped the practice claiming that both he and his wife would have sooner entered the workhouse than continue subjecting the child to such misery.

The master sweep went on to give an extremely candid description of the process and the suffering involved by the younger boys:

'No one knows the cruelty which a boy has to undergo in learning. The flesh must be hardened. This is done by rubbing it, chiefly on the elbows and knees and with the strongest brine, as that got from a pork-shop, close by a hot fire. You must stand over them with a cane, or coax them by a promise of a halfpenny, etc. if they will stand a few more rubs. At first they will come back from their work with their arms and knees streaming with blood, and the knees looking as if the caps had been pulled off. They must be rubbed with brine again, and perhaps, go off at once to another chimney. In some boys I have heard that the flesh does not harden for years.'

Whilst certain sections of society clearly opposed the use of boys in this work it was also obvious that many were quite happy with the practice, including some magistrates who, ironically, should have enforced the law against child sweeps. One instance of a magistrates reluctance to prosecute, the case of a boy presented to the court after having been seen at work within a chimney, resulted in an acquittal for the master on the grounds that the boy could not offer strict proof of his being less than 21 years of age. He was described as being no more than nine or ten years old by the prosecutor and was present, as mentioned, for the court to see. The Coroner for Nottingham also added in his evidence to the Commissioners that during the hearing outlined above, it was proven that the presiding magistrate had chimneys in his own house that could only be swept by boys and not machines.

Further information from two inquests held by Mr. Michael Brown, solicitor and coroner to Nottingham, revealed other details of the ruthless exploitation of young children.

'I remember two inquests which I have held, on deaths of climbing boys in chimneys. In one case when the master came with his boy to sweep the chimney the fire was still burning, and had to be put out, and something put over the still hot iron of the fire-place, to enable the boy to rest his feet upon at starting. I attributed his death in this case partly to the air in the chimney, having not had time to become fit for breathing, so that exhaustion was more likely to follow. A hole was broken in the wall to get the boy out. In the other case, the master had lit straw under the chimney to bring the boy down, as he (the master) thought the boy was alseep, when in reality he was dead. These facts were proved before me.'

A chimney sweep from Burslem, Staffordshire, told the Commissioners that in Leicester, since 1840, 23 boys had been killed 'by being stifled' this same chimney sweep also stated that there was not a single climbing boy in 'The Potteries', the reason being that there were 'many good gentlemen there to put it down'. Inspectors, magistrates and the police were vigilant with the result that offending housekeepers were fined £5 and sweeps sentenced to gaol for periods of one or two months.

The 'Birmingham Association for the Suppression of the Use of Climbing Boys' was formed in 1856. It was reported that over a five year period to 1861 a sum of nearly £500 was spent in the borough in the effort to prevent the use of climbing boys. A Midland Association for the Suppression of the Climbing System was also formed in January 1857 with the intention of covering the counties of Leicestershire, Derby, Nottingham, Northampton and part of Warwickshire. The intention was to make every effort to carry out the law against the use of climbing boys but it was also pointed out that the Association, before entering on prosecutions spent a considerable sum of money on advertising 'so that by the press and other means the public might be well informed, and an opportunity be given to the men to dismiss the boys and conform to the law.' From

The Sweeps' Home, again taken from Mayhew's 'London labour and the London Poor', 1861. The description of much accommodation for sweeps in the pages of the Commissioner's reports suggest a far less salubrious environment than shown here.

1 March 1856 all master sweeps in the County of Leicester were given sweeping machines in return for the written promise that in each case they would refrain from employing climbing boys. The cost of the machines amounted to £147. Despite such innovations, many sweeps continued to use boys making it necessary to prosecute. In certain cases boys were sold within the county and taken away to other parts of the country to continue work.

The treasurer of the Midland Association, a magistrate himself, gave a written account of the practice whereby children were sold to sweeps in other parts of the country: 'From the fact that have come to my knowledge I am satisfied that great numbers of these children are regularly bought and sold; andthat practicably they are as completely slaves as any negro children in South Carolina'. In 1861 a man and woman were charged before themagistrate of Leicester for having conspired to obtain two illegitimate children, of the age of 6 and 8 years, under false pretences from the workhouse. The children were taken to Grantham toa chimney sweeper, but were fortunately recovered.From the evidence it seems that climbing boys began their work betweenthe ages of six and eight years, although in Nottingham a child was atwork at the age of four. His age was actually verified by his father,who, having named him to the chimney sweep, added that he would make 'a nice little climber'.

Work often started early in the morning before fires were needed. In Nottingham, George Ruff stated that work began at or about 4-4.30 am and lasted for 12 hours. James Brown a journeyman chimney sweeper of Winchester claimed that in the country areas he started work with his boy at 3 or even 2 am and sometimes continued until 9 or 10 pm.

Being fed, clothed and disciplined by their masters, the climbing boys enjoyed little in the way of even basic comforts. Many would, inevitably, 'sleep black', and washing very infrequently. The nature of the work without doubt brought early death and disease to these young people. Instances have been given of boys being killed whilst at their work, but many more suffered the effects of the 'sooty cancer'. In the words of one Nottinghamshire sweep:

'There is no cure for it when once begun.'

Looking back at his own early experience, Richard Stansfield, a sweep in Manchester related the problem of dirt and disease made worse by the wretched living conditions endured by the boys:

'I have gone to bed with my knee and elbow scabbed and raw, and the inside of my thighs all scarified; we slept 5 or 6 boys together in a sort of cellar with the soot bags over us, sticking in the sounds sometimes; that and some straw were all our bed and bedclothes – they were the same bags we had used in the day, wet or dry. I could read, and we used sometimes to subscribe for a candle to read by when we were in bed. I have seen the steam from our bodies so thick as to obscure the light so that I couldn't read at all. Dozens die of consumption; they get up about their work in all weathers and often at 2 or 3 am. They are filthy in their habits; lads often wear one shirt right on till it is done with. I have been for 15 months without being washed, except by the rain.'

Together with their wretched physical/material condition, the climbing boys also enjoyed little in the way of any positive moral environment. Many master sweeps spoke of members of their trade as being no more than illiterate, selfish, brutal and narrow in their outlook. Nor surprisingly, the boys also became accustomed to such a way of life.

In evidence of the Children's Employment Commissioners, Peter Hall of Stockport, an agent for the 'North Staffordshire and Birmingham Association for preventing the Employment of Climbing Boys,' said the following:

'It is rare for climbing boys to get any other than a Sunday School education and very few get that from my knowledge. Generally speaking they are brought up in gross ignorance and vice, they don't go to evening school as they don't take the trouble to wash themselves. They have not been accustomed to education when young and they don't think of it. When I took the statistics of them in 1851, out of 348 boys, I could only find 6 of them who could write, and 26 who could read, and most of them very imperfectly. I have not a shadow of a doubt from my frequent communication with them that they are not only in the same state of ignorance now, but even worse, because the masters who bring up these children to climbing now are the worst in the trade so far.'

Looking to a somewhat different source, one could well refer to Charles Kingsley's novel, The Water Babies. First published in 1863, the author must have been more than familiar with the debate over the use of children as sweeps. Kingsley's description of Tom, the climbing boy, echoes much of what was reported to the Commissioners from 1862:

'He could not read or write, and did not care to do either; and he never washed himself, for there was no water up the court where he lived. He had never heard of God or Christ. He cried half his time and laughed the other half.'

The Children's Employment Commission recorded its reason for the apparent failure of the Act of 1840 and for the continued use of the boys as chimney sweeps. Four basic points were made:

1. The general apathy or active prejudices of the householders.
2. The want of efficient machinery for putting the Act into operation.
3. The disinclination of magistrates to convict.
4. Defects in the Act itself, and the difficulty of proving the offence.

The report ended with the publication of the following measures, suggested as appropriate to the problems under investigation.

1. That no person using the trade of a chimney sweep shall be permitted to employ in his business in any capacity whatever any person under the age of 16, whether as an apprentice or otherwise.
2. That the clause of the Act referred to relative to the proper construction of chimneys, the introduction of 'soot holes', etc. should be made more stringent by requiring that the plans of all new houses should be approved of by the proper local authority and by rendering the architect responsible as well as the builder for any violation of the law.
3. That no person should be allowed to carry on the trade of a chimney sweeper until he has received a licence from the magistrates or other competent authority.
4. That it should make a part of the duty of the police to make inquiry as to whether the provisions of the Act of Parliament are attended to in their respective districts, and to take proceedings where requisite for enforcing the Act.
5. That in all cases were journeyman sweepers are lodged by their employers, suitable sanitary arrangements to ensure cleanliness and prevent disease should be enforced by the officers of the Board of Health or other local authorities.
6. According to the existing Act, imprisonment can only be inflicted on default of payment on any penalty that may have been awarded for the violation of the law. But there are some cases of excess cruelty, involving even danger to life, as for instance at Ashton-under-Lyne, where a child 7 years old was severely burnt by being sent up a chimney on fire. We submit therefore that it would, in the interests of humanity, be proper that the magistrate should be empowered, if he sees fit, in cases where cruelty or ill treatment has been proved, to inflict imprisonment, with or without hard labour, for any time not exceeding two months, the limit prescribed by the Act instead of imposing a penalty.

The final point referred to the actual amount set as a fine. The Commissioners, mindful of the fact that magistrates were often reluctant to impose the existing £5 fine, concluded that a penalty of between £2 (40 shillings) and £10 be introduced.

With these recommendations and the untiring efforts of Lord Shaftesbury, champion of the climbing boys' cause, a Bill 'to amend and extend the Act for the Regulation of Chimney Sweepers' was introduced into the House of Lords. It became law on 30 June 1864.

The Act was obviously an improvement where it was taken seriously by the community, but, once again, it failed to solve the problem of the abuse of young children by sweeps, of the

indifference of society looking to its own interest and the lack of vigilant action by the police to enforce measures. Unlike the examples of Glasgow and Edinburgh, where sweeps had to have licences, were required by law to display an official badge and were subject to detailed scrutiny by the police, no such measures were included in the 1864 legislation.

Giving evidence, once again to the commissioners in April 1866, Peter Hall, on behalf of the Midland, North Staffordshire and Birmingham Associations included the following:

'In all large towns in England the employment of climbing boys is on the increase; in particular in Birmingham notwithstanding many prosecutions. I have had at least 50 prosecutions in Birmingham within the last seven years; nevertheless the system is on the increase. There are now 25 boys employed; their ages range from 5 to 10 years. They are on the increase in Liverpool and Manchester. There are several also at Preston, Oldham, Staleybridge and Ashton; in Dudley, Wolverhampton and all the Black Country; at Nottingham and Mansfield. At Derby they are also on the increase and at Worcester, Grantham, Boston and several other towns that I could mention. To my knowledge many of these young boys are employed by their own parents.'

Peter Hall put forward what he considered were two absolutely essential proposals to strengthen the existing Act. They were, firstly, that no person should be allowed to carry on the business of a sweep without a licence, and, secondly, that it should be made the duty of the police to enforce the Act. As with all legislation that did not carry effective enforcement, the 1864 Act went unheeded except for the work of those dedicated to its success.

Above and below: Two examples of other forms of employment for young people on the London streets – the crossing-sweepers and the link-boys, guiding people through fog or, at other times, providing light at night.

Further legislation followed in 1875 when, finally, Peter Hall's proposals were included in the Act. This brought England into line with the existing legislation covering Glasgow and Edinburgh. Being clearly licenced and closely monitored by the police, the chimney sweep could no longer afford to openly ignore the law and submit young children to the horrors of the chimney.

Chapter Seven
The Lace Industry

Whilst mining was an important industry in West Devon, lace manufacture, a very different form of occupation, provided employment in the east of the county. Pillow lace making was widespread in the Honiton district and amongst the towns and villages along the coast. The industry was organised around the traditional pattern of 'cottage' production based on the home. Lace-making 'schools' were long established features of the industry where children learned the work as apprentices of sorts. Under supervision, they worked in groups gathered in accommodation perhaps at the back or to the side of a cottage, or, indeed, in one of the rooms within the house itself.

Evidence from the Childrens' Employment Commission, 1862, revealed harsh conditions within Devon's lace-making industry, despite its would-be idyllic associations today. Pillow lace-making was described by reference to a lace manufacturer in Honiton itself:

'Mrs. Godolphin takes orders from wholesale houses and warehouses or private families, gives out patterns to the lacemakers, and sells them their thread. The lacemakers work in their own homes or in schools. The lace is made on pillows, in small separate pieces or 'sprigs', some extremely small, and made by the dozen which are brought back to her, and are then 'made up' by joining them together, whether on the pillow by lace, or by the needle, or by sewing them onto net. Unless very busy has this done in her own house. It is considered the best part of the work, and the best paid, and is generally done by young women, children not being suitable for it. Girls might learn this at 12 years old, but they go to learn lace-making at 5 or 6 years, and many towards 7. They usually go as apprentices

Pillow lace-making. Girls began work, lace-making, from as early as five years old. Poor eye sight, frequent headaches and long-term physical deformity was common amongst lace girls. Extremely long hours in closely confined surroundings, added to the fact that the girls were frequently obliged to take payment in 'truck goods', made this cottage industry a much less attractive proposition than might be imagined today. Gloving, and other related activities – the seamstress and shirt makers, for example – shared many of the problems of this demanding, sedentary employment.

for three years, paying nothing and getting nothing, except perhaps after a time, a garment once a quarter, and not paying for the lace they spoil.'

Girls made up the bulk of the work-force in the lace-making industry as the Rev. J. A. Mackurness, Rector of Honiton, stated:

'Most of the young females in the town, the population of which is 3,300, are engaged in lace-making and as a consequence leave school early, ie. at about 7 or 8 years old.'

This requirement to take girls at such an early age clearly damaged the process of education. The schoolmistress at Seaton Infants School, for example, was unable to keep girls at lessons as the Royal Commission explained:

'Miss Coles is mistress of the infant school here, supported by a lady, at which boys may be kept till 9 years old, and girls till 10, for the weekly payment of 1d., or ½d. if there be more than one child of the same family. There are about 60 girls and boys in equal numbers, but there are not more than a dozen girls above 7 years old in the school.'

A similar situation applied at Seaton's elementary school, where the number of girls, from 20 to 25, was only half that of the boys. The Rev. Cradock Gluscott, vicar of Seaton and Beer, was very forthright on the subject, underlining the consequence of girls' early entry into work and the inevitable lack of education that followed:

'They grow up untaught, and ignorant of plain household duties such as sewing, washing, etc., and this makes it difficult to get situations in service for them, though I endeavour to do so; and when they marry, as they do very early, they are quite unfit for it, and unable to nurse and bring up their children properly. The children not being taught obedience, there is but little parental authority.'

An idyllic mid-Victorian village scene to be found in most parts of Britain. Such communities frequently housed cottage industries such as the lace-makers of East Devon or the glovers of Somerset. Conditions within these two particular domestic industries often ran counter to their would-be appearance. Within these houses, girls worked long hours in extremely unpleasant conditions.

The Rev. gentleman also went on to emphasise two other important questions; the extremely bad working conditions and the widespread use of the truck system in payment. Both these will be considered here in more detail.

An obvious instance of the hopelessly inadequate and unregulated working conditions is seen in the case of a Mrs. Besley's Lace School at Seaton. The Commissioners' report read as follows:

'When I first entered this school the girls had left for dinner, but the room was offensively close, and though the day was fine and mild the window was not opened in the interval. The room, which is built on to the back of the cottage apparently for the purpose, as it is much like some other lace schools which I have seen, opens only into a passage, is nearly square, a little over 330 cubic feet, and there is no fireplace or means of warming. The average number of scholars is seven, and three grown-up daughters of the mistress also work here. The entire number working together has been 12, but it was not stated whether this ever happened in the small room. In summer, the large living room is used. Twelve people in the small room would have 28 cubic feet of space each.

MRS. MARY BESLEY witness. Takes about seven girls, more or less, from 6 years old upwards, which is the usual age for beginning lace, some as apprentices who for a year and a half give their work for their teaching, and afterwards pay 4d. a week, and have their own lace. They are set 10 hours work, ie. about from 7 am to 7 pm in summer, with hours for breakfast, dinner and tea, and from 8 am to 8 pm in winter, with meals. But sometimes in winter they cannot do half a day's work on account of the cold, and in summer they are hindered by their hands being so warm and sticky. They will not be able to work in the small room much longer (ie. than the beginning of February), because it is so close. They never work out of doors, even in the summer. Girls, as soon as they have left lace school, and young women work all day, and they like to do so away from home, as they do not get so much talking to from their mothers.

MARIA BESLEY. Is daughter to last witness. Learned lace-making at home at 6 years old. Some put their children to it at 5, but she wonders they have the heart to do so. One of that age at school with her went for four hours a day at first, and after a year from 8½ am till 5 pm. Generally begins work now after breakfast, ie. between 8 and 9 o'clock, and works till 10 pm; but this winter she has worked many times till 11½ and 12 pm, and in summer till 4 and 5 in the morning and sometimes all through the night, without going to bed, or stopping at all, except just to take anything in (to eat). Dare say she was 16 when she first sat at work all through the night. (Looks but little above that now). Other girls in the place work and sit up in the same way (her sister confirms this). Is obliged to work as hard as this, and is glad to do so. 'This work tries any one's head.' Has headaches: they are common among lace-makers. It also tries the eyes, and sometimes they cannot get on at all by candle light. One 'eight' (ie. 8 to the lb.) dip candle serves for three of the big workers to sit round, and for four of the younger girls who make plainer work.

EMILY WESTLAKE, age 13. Began lace-making at 7 years old, and was at a week day school for a year before that, and goes to Sunday School. Knows the letters (and no more), but no figures (when shown) except '1'. (The sister of this girl, aged 9, did not begin lace till 8, and can spell).

Payment in 'truck' was a widely accepted practice in the lace-making district, but was disliked by the employees. The truck system was the payment of wages not in money, but in goods. It obviously favoured the employer and offered the opportunity for dishonesty and corruption at every stage. Operating on a monopoly basis, payment in truck often entailed high prices for inferior goods. The system also encouraged dependence upon the employer, by taking away the possibility of workers saving money to begin their own business or to simply shop elsewhere for goods. The vicar of Seaton also emphasised the threat to public morality posed by truck payment. As the girls were obliged to accept part of their wage in clothes the minister noted that they dressed 'very showily' thereby encouraging, it seems, all manner of problems within their community!'

Mrs. Harriet Wheeker of Sidbury described the working of the truck system and its effects:

'The worst fault is that the lace shops get the profits of the work. Nearly all lace manufacturers in the neighbourhood keep general shops, and make the lace-makers take goods for money, though I have heard of one of the large dealers who pays half in money. They will only give out these goods on certain days, as once or twice a week, the days here being, I believe, Wednesday and Saturday, and then not what the lace-maker wish, but what they, the manufacturers, like to allow and think needed for actual use. Thus two loaves of bread and ½lb. of butter form part of a common weekly allowance to girls. The object of this is to prevent the people from selling the goods again and so getting any ready money, which would enable them to be independent, and buy anything which they might wish for at other shops where they could get better. Sometimes a manufacturer actually refuses something that is asked for on the ground that it cannot be wanted for use but for sale. The other day a girl, who had been working long hours to earn more, came and asked me if I would buy from her a pound of white sugar for 6½d. if she could get it, 6½d. being the proper market price, though the price of this sugar would be put down to the girl herself at 8d. Still for the sake of the ready money she wished to do this, but was unable to get the sugar, the manufacturer saying that she did not need it for her own use. On the same grounds manufacturers are very jealous of their girls working over hours for anyone else, and will ask a girl what she had a light so late at night for. Sometimes a few girls, say four, will club together to make a collar or something, and get a few shillings in money by selling it privately, but if they are found out in this they are turned out of employment by the shop. The lace-makers feel this very much, and I have seen them even crying because they are not allowed to get any money. Besides this, it is expected that the other members of the family shall buy their goods at the shop to which the girl's lace is taken. An instance of this occurred just lately when

A rather sentimentalised view of Dame School, obviously in a rural location. Allowing for the charming setting here, with its friendly garden scene and cosy cottage interior, the illustration gives some idea of the nature of education, its expectations and obvious limitation for children such as this in the period of the mid century.

complaint was made of a child, who had been sent on an errand, being seen to enter another shop. I heard a mother complain lately of one manufacturer being so exacting in such ways that her children should never work for this shop again 'if she could help it.' In addition to this the goods are charged to the lace-makers at unfair prices. I know of boots bought at a shop for 5s. a pair being sold to the lace girls for 10s. 6d., and of other cases of the same kind. Every article is charged against the lace-maker at her shop (ie. that to which she takes her lace) something over the price paid by other people. Calico which I get for 7d. would be 9d. or 10d. to a lace girl; lump sugar instead of 6½d. the lb. would be 8d.; candles ditto; bacon is always 1d. or 2d. a pound dearer to them; and other things in like manner, and all the year round.

I wish that the Government could do something to stop this: it is so cruel. I could myself if I had the capital to spare.

Any shop that would pay ready money and sell on fair terms would make a fortune, and it would be much better for all.'

Improved conditions for young people followed gradually from the 1860s. Prompted by the findings of the Children's Employment Commission which investigated wide ranging forms of employment between 1862 and 1866, Parliament passed the Factory Acts of 1864 and 1867. The 1867 Act said that no child under the age of 8 should be allowed to work whilst other children were to be given at least 10 hours schooling each week. A further Act of 1878 brought improvement mainly by consolidating all earlier Acts, clarifying procedure, and abolishing the difficult distinctions between factories and workshops.

The development of elementary education, seen as a crucial issue by the early 1870s, also brought improvements for children. Forster's Education Act of 1870 marking for the determination to provide a national system of elementary schooling was an important landmark, but it was not until 1880 that education was finally made compulsory for all children between the ages of 5 and 10. Free schooling came in 1891. All Factory Acts had the effect of increasing the place of education in children's lives; likewise, every Education Act had the effect of gradually removing children from early employment. With cottage style production in decline due to mechanisation elsewhere, a factor noted by the Commission, and the strengthening of legislation to protect children, the lace industry in Devon changed considerably in structure and extent in the second half of the nineteenth century.

Chapter Eight
The Cocklers – Morecambe Bay

Included amongst the work of the 'Commission on the Employment of Young Children, young Persons and Women In Agriculture' (1867) was a report on the cocklers living along the shores of Morecambe Bay. The investigation came as part of the general report covering the northern district of Lancashire and gave valuable insights into the circumstances of the cockle-gathering communities and their dependence upon the daily work on the sands.

The young women and children employed to gather the cockles were organised and supervised, by men known locally as 'badgers'. Working in groups of 10 to 20 the gatherers searched beneath the sands at low tide with their small three-pronged forks called 'crams' removing the cockles. For a 'heap' of cockles, amounting to eight quarts, the children would receive 5d.; the cockles were then sold by the 'badgers' at a rate of 2d. per quart.

Fresh cockles were gathered, bagged and sent by rail to the manufacturing towns of South Lancashire. The Stationmaster at Morecambe informed the Assistant Commissioner that the movement of cockles and mussels from his station alone brought the railway an income of more than £2000 per year. Dealers in the large towns and cities arranged for consignments on a daily basis and thereby guaranteed continuous employment for the large numbers of people scattered around Morecambe Bay. Entire families were devoted to cockling for which they received considerable returns, amounting to as much as 12 shillings for a day's work on a family basis.

Giving evidence to the Assistant Commissioners, the Rev. Rigg, incumbent of Flookborough, related:

'This is one of the principal villages on the shore of Morecambe Bay, and is inhabited chiefly by fishermen and by a class of people called 'cocklers'. At least 100 boys, girls and women go on the sands daily, and sometimes twice a day to collect cockles. The children employed go upon the sands as young as 7 or 8, consequently they get no education whatsoever, rarely

Lancaster Sands and Morecambe Bay seen from the high ground overlooking the county town. The sands were the setting for the cocklers who made their living on this dangerous, open expanse, working from numerous small communities around the bay. Infants, only four years of age, were also employed in the surrounding villages potting shrimps gathered on the sands. The vast tidal expanse was a place of considerable danger, both to those working there, and those attempting to find their way across it in the course of a journey. In the spring of 1857, for example, a group of some 10 to 13 young people, farm labourers and female household servants, were caught by the incoming tide and drowned whilst on their way to a hiring fair at Lancaster.

A shrimp gatherer, 1868. The Illustrated London News offered the following caption for this particular study: "This picture may suggest a momentary feeling of sympathy for the myriads of our lowly brethren and sisters who face lives of drudgery and, totally sacrificing health, sometimes, as well as comfort to place on our tables some scarcely heeded little crustacea or other appetizing delicacy."

even going to the infant school. The children and young persons engaged in this business are in a very demoralised condition, they never enter a place of worship and their language when idling about the streets is disgusting. Tasking the eight or nine villages on the shore of Morecambe Bay there must be several hundreds of children who, owing to this cockling business, are growing up in a state of heathenism.'

Unlike the brickfields, for example, where work was limited to the summer months, cockling could be carried out throughout the year, and, whereas some of the worst influences of life in the brickfields could be offset by children attending school during the winter months, no such situation applied to the children on the sands. At the age of 14 the children, according to the Rev. Rigg's account, often left their parent's homes, and, becoming quite independent, lodged with strangers and spent their money in drunkenness.

Two pieces of evidence from those closely associated with the cockling trade offer further details on the nature of this employment. A Mrs. Butler of Flookborough declared:

'I have three girls now on the sands. They are generally absent from home 10 or 12 hours together; in spring tides they have to walk five miles to the banks, which, with a mile to the shore, makes 12 miles going and returning, besides cockling for five hours. They are a bit tired when they come home, and are quite ready for a meal; they have nothing on the sands, but a piece of bread, of which they eat a bit now and then just to keep off the hunger. It is a slavish life, but what are poor people to do? My girls went to the infant school until the were 8, but they have not been to any school since; they cannot read.'

Mr. Burrows, another member of the community at Flookborough emphasised the harsh conditions faced by the children involved:

'I have four boys on the sands today; they went at 4 this morning, and will return at 4 this afternoon. They have never been to school. Cockling children must begin early; little things 5 years old go out a little to help and learn. They get a lift in the carts. A good bit of the work is walking. The children live chiefly on tea and bread.'

The Rev. Macaulay, rector of Adlingham, could report that no children worked in the fields within his district, but he drew attention to the situation of the cocklers. He pointed out that the

earnings were so considerable that it was too much to expect that parents would resist the temptation to employ their children. Speaking of the children's condition he described them as 'rough in manners, and their language is very coarse'. Like many others who expressed concern for the children, he looked to the possibility of an enforced period of full-time education and an age limit for the work.

In support of his colleague, the Rev. Can Hubbersty, vicar of Cartmel, described cockling as 'the only abuse of children's labour that we have to complain of in this district'. Taking the somewhat more expedient view on employment, a farmer from Ulverstone, Mr. Richard Presowe, stated:

'We cannot get women to work out here; their husbands are too well off. The children make more by cockling than they could be working in the fields.'

Almost by way of final reference to the children's employment around Morecambe Bay, the Rev. Manby, rector of Poulton-le-Sands, described the work of much younger children in related activities. He maintained that, for the greater part of the day, infants of only four years of age were to be seen seated around tables preparing shrimps for potting. This, it was stated, was a common sight and one for which the children could receive from 6d. to 9d. per day.

The final reference to the practice of gathering cockles, and, with it, a statement on the impact that this employment had upon the community generally, is that of the Rev. J. D. Bannister, vicar of Pilling near Fleetwood.

'Cockling was formerly carried on from this place to a great extent, but the cockles have dispersed, to the great benefit of the parish, morally and intellectually.'

Fortunately, for the working population, the vicar could also report that a day labourer could earn a weekly wage of 18 shillings. 'The labouring classes', he wrote, 'are remarkably well off and there is no poverty'.

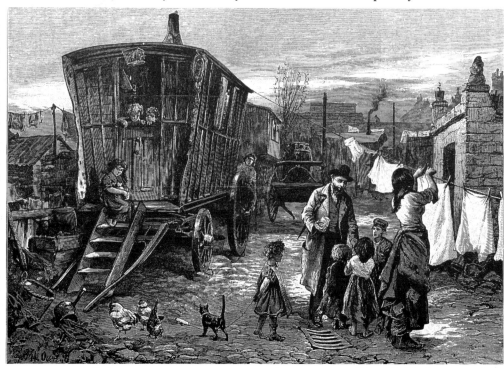

Above and previous page: Gypsy society was also the subject of investigation and concern by the 1870s, particularly the state of the children and their prospects for later, adult life. Mr George Smith of Coalville, Leicestershire, focused considerable attention on the circumstances of gypsy life. By the late 1870s, gypsies, together with other elements of the semi-nomadic community, such as the canal or barge people, were recognised as being neglected sections of society, often isolated and acutely deprived socially. In the course of his benevolent efforts on their part, George Smith attempted to obtain legislation to cover aspects of gypsy life, and help remedy the sad neglect with regard to children's circumstances, domestic comfort, health and eduction. To illustrate and emphasise his case, George Smith warned of some 10 to almost 15 thousand gypsy children "moving about the countryside outside the eduction laws and the pale of civilization." In London, the main districts for gypsy encampments were Notting Hill and Barnes Common, together with Wormwood Scrubs. The worst district was that between Shepherd's Bush and Notting Hill, where the camp adjoined brickfields, waste land and new building sites. Drawing on stark comparisons, emphasising the irony, Smith wrote of the gypsy settlements with their level of neglect, as something to the shame of British society. "In these places, children are born, live and die. Men, women and children, grown up sons and daughters huddle together in such a state as would shock the modesty of South African savages to whom we send missionaries to show them the blessings of Christianity." The moral imperative apparent here bore a definite similarity to the manner and means of those active in the movement for reform in the mines and mills earlier in the century. In the two views here, one shows an interior scene inside a van near Latimer Road, Notting Hill. The tent was home to two men and their wives, together with their 14 children. The second view shows George Smith in the company of small children outside a gypsy van.

Chapter Nine
The Mud-Larks
... the most deplorable in appearance of any I have met with ...

Henry Mayhew's 'London Labour and London Poor,' published in 1861, included an account of the young mud-larks of the River Thames. Mud-larks spent their days scavenging amongst the mud of the river as and when the tide allowed. Their story, as gathered by Mayhew, presents us with a vivid picture of life for these children at work during the mid-century. It is story of hardship and neglect.

The mud-larks lived in the courts and alleys making up many of the riverside communities and each day they gathered in groups to wade into the mud as the tide fell. Given the foul state of the Thames at that time and the wretched condition of their housing and general environment, their way of life could amount to no more than a daily struggle for existence. Indeed, one mud-lark told Mayhew of his preference for prison life as an alternative to the mud banks.

Mud-larks collected whatever was considered valuable. Such items included wood, bones, pieces of iron, old clothes, and rags, and, most prized of all, other than actual money itself, copper nails from ships. These items would then be sold either to individuals or to the rag shops enabling the mud-lark to earn something between 2Åd. and 8d. for their day's work. An income of 3d. per day was considered the usual return.

The children, and adults also, were to be found at their business all along the river from Vauxhall Bridge to Woolwich. The section of river from Execution Dock to Limehouse Hole offered fourteen flights of stairs and landing places giving easy access to the mud and the likelihood of useful discoveries. The ship yards in the districts of Greenwich, Deptford and Woolwich also provided the mud-larks with the opportunity to find valuable items linked with the work of the yards. They searched in small groups independent of others along the river, invariably working in silence, being very uncommunicative people. Mayhew described the children as 'dull and apparently stupid', who when engaged in searching the mud, hold but little converse one with another'.

A somewhat idealised illustration of the famous Thames mudlarks. These boys (and girls) were described by Henry Mayhew as "the most deplorable in appearance of any I have met with."

As regards their general appearance Mayhew was forthright:

'They may be seen of all ages from mere childhood to positive decrepitude, crawling among the barges at the various wharfs along the river; it cannot be said that they are clad in rags, for they are scarcely half covered by the tattered indescribable things which serve for them as clothes; their bodies were grimed with the foul soil of the river, and their torn garments stiffened up like boards with dirt of every possible description.'

His verdict upon their conditions was summoned up in one sentence:

'These poor creatures are certainly about the most deplorable in their appearance of any I have met within the course of my enquiries.' Given the scope of Mayhew's investigations and the manner of people encountered amongst the poor the mud-larks' situation must, indeed, have been desperate for him to have made such a definite statement as this.

The mud-larks related their circumstances to Mayhew who drew the inevitable conclusion that there was 'a painful uniformity in the stories of all these children'.

They were either the children of the very poor, who, by their own improvidence or some overwhelming calamity, had been reduced to the extremity of distress, or else they were orphans, and compelled, from utter destitution, to seek for the means of appeasing their hunger in the mud of the river. 'That the majority of this class are ignorant, and without even the rudiments of education, and that many of them from time to time are committed to prison for petty thefts, cannot be wondered at.'

Many of the mud-larks openly declare their preference for prison life over that on the mud banks. The boys told of their being fed, clothed and sheltered in prison in a way that was vastly superior to anything they could possibly hope for in their normal lives.

Mayhew's observations on young girls exposed to the riverside environment were especially distressing:

'Waifs and strays of London', as recorded by the Illustrated London News in the 1880s. Such children, once discovered and claimed, would be subject to the attention of the school boards to provide for their education.

'As for the females growing up under such circumstances the worst may be anticipated of them and in proof of this I have found, on inquiry, that very many of the unfortunate creatures who swell the time of prostitution in Ratcliff-highway, and some other low neighbourhoods in the East of London, have originally been mud-larks; and only remained at that occupation till such time as they were capable of adopting the more easy and lucrative life of the prostitute.'

With direct reference to one of the young people encountered by Mayhew it is possible to construct a fairly detailed, representative view of the situation. The writer intended to emphasise his conviction that the poor were degraded by their circumstances and also deprived of the opportunity to demonstrate their potential to be 'respectable members of society'.

'The lad of whom I speak was discovered by me now nearly two years ago 'mud-larking' on the banks of the river near the docks. He was a quick, intelligent little fellow, and had been at the business about three years. He had taken to mud-larking because his clothes were too bad for him to look for anything better. He worked every day with 20 or 30 boys, who might be seen at daybreak with their trousers tucked up groping about, and picking out the pieces of coal from the mud on the bank of the Thames. He went into the river up to his knees and in searching the mud he often ran pieces of glass and long nails into his feet. When this was the case he went home and dressed the wounds, but returned to the riverside directly, 'for should the tide come up,' he added 'without my having found something, why, I must starve till the next low tide.' In the very cold weather he and his other shoeless companion used to stand in the hot water that ran down the river side from some of the steam factories to warm their frozen feet.

The boy was fourteen years old and related how he had experiences both comfortable and difficult times including being sent to school regularly and, by contrast, extreme poverty and illness. In circumstances of dire poverty the boy returned to the river in order to provide for his mother and himself, his mother being seriously ill.'

Mayhew then related how the boy suffered injuries from broken glass and nails and how he eventually made contact with the Ragged School movement, through classes held at High Street, Wapping. The boy himself continued his story explaining how other boys encouraged him to attend the school:

Two illustrations of the Lambeth Ragged School, showing separate classes for boys and girls. The Ragged Schools Union was formed in 1844 with Shaftesbury as its Chairman. It did a great deal to help those otherwise doomed to a life of utter wretchedness. As Dickens put it, ragged schools intended "to introduce amongst the most miserable and neglected outcasts, some knowledge of the commonest principles of morality and religion. The attempt is being made in certain more obscure and squalid parts of the metropolis, where rooms are opened at night for all comers...they who are too ragged, wretched, filthy or forlorn to enter any other place."

Two views of Brooke Street Ragged School, London (1853) showing the school room and the work room. Brooke Street was a particular success. The Ragged School Union also met with success in its policy of promoting emigration amongst the poor as their best prospect for all-round improvement.

'They asked me to come along with them for it was great fun. They told that all the boys used to be laughing and making game of the master. They said they used to put out the gas and chuck the slates about. They told me, too, that there was a good fire there, so I went to have a warm and see what it was like. When I got there the master was very kind to me. They used to give us tea-parties, and to keep us quiet they used to show us the magic lantern. I soon got to like going there, and went every night for six months. There was about 40 to 50 boys in the school. The most of them were thieves, and they used to go thieving the coals out of barges along the shore and cutting the ropes off ships and going and selling it at the rag shops.'

Quite apart from the boy's story this extract offers an interesting insight into conditions within the Ragged Schools and the problem encountered by teaching staff faced with an almost impossible task. It also stresses, however, the gradual impact of education upon the boy.

A cartoon from 'Punch' emphasising the advantages of emigration, contrasting the deprivation and misery in Britain with the opportunities for comfort and well-being overseas. 'Punch' also cautions against involvements with Socialism or Chartism, indicated by reference to the notices on the wall. The working people were better advised here to avoid such movements, and seek-out emigration as the means to well-being.

Continuing his story, the boy told how he became involved in the criminal activities of his young colleagues, but most significantly, Mayhew ends the account by reporting that he, himself, helped the boy obtain a situation in the printing trade. Mayhew was able to see his young friend secure a situation in one of the daily newspaper offices with his wages increasing from six to nine shillings a week.

The story, of course, reflects the Victorian concern for self improvement through education, hard work and resol-

ute character but it served to illustrate Mayhew's main point. He was particularly anxious to show through such a story that, given the opportunity, many more of these unfortunate, neglected young people would also have made their way in the world. To survive at all on the mud banks was itself something of a testimony to endurance, and, with little alternative means of support, their work could well be described as enterprising, despite its wretched circumstances.

Children and teachers at the National School, Plaistow, in the neighbourhood of London's Victoria Docks. Described as the cheapest school in England, its ramshackle wooden structure was host to up to 200 children at different times. The teacher's salary was £35 per year. Such circumstances serve to offer perspective on the actual condition and quality of eduction provided for poor children across the country. Such institutions as this, together with the work of the Ragged Schools, accomplished all that they could on behalf of numerous deprived and exploited young people within their area.

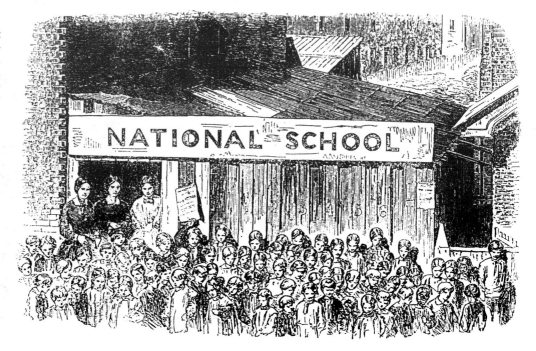

Indication of the work carried out at the Nichol Street Ragged School, Shoreditch in the interest of children's welfare, 1886.

Chapter Ten
Child Prostitution

Passing reference to prostitution has been made with regard to the girls working as mud-larks on the Thames. It was also suspected and feared, albeit on a casual and opportunist basis, in many other forms of employment. Child prostitution in a blatant form was, nevertheless, a reality throughout Britain during the 19th century; a fact of life, however distasteful, then or now.

Evidence to a Select Committee on Law relating to the Protection of Young Girls, 1881, revealed conditions in London. The Director of Criminal Investigations, Mr. Howard-Vincent, addressed the situation:

'There are houses in London, in many parts of London, where there are people who will procure children for the purposes of immorality and prostitution, without any difficulty whatsoever above the age of 13 and children without number at 14, 15 and 16 years of age. Juvenile prostitution is rampant at this moment, and that in the streets about Haymarket, Waterloo Place and Piccadilly, from nightfall there are children openly soliciting prostitution. Now it constantly happens and I believe in the generality of cases it is so that these children live at home; this prostitution actually takes place with the knowledge and connivance of the mother and to the profit of the household.'

In his evidence to the Committee, Mr. Daniel Morgan, an inspector in C.I.D. X Division, Paddington, stated that many young girls took to prostitution 'spontaneously'. Having seen the greatly enhanced material circumstances of older friends and acquaintances the younger girls inevitably emulated them. Describing his experience the Inspector made reference to the Marylebone and Pentonville Hill districts:

The wallflower girl from Henry Mayhew's 'London Life and london labour.' Girls such as this, selling their various wares could often find themselves drawn into the inevitable circumstances of casual prostitution when beset with the problem of existence on the streets. The sad but stark facts of life made them special targets for all manner of undesirables, eager to find young girls without the likelihood of being diseased, and who would provide cheap satisfaction for those seeking to support them.

'In Marylebone and Pentonville Hill especially I should think it scarcely possible for anyone between 9 pm and 1 am to walk along Pentonville Hill without being accosted by about a dozen young girls between 13 and 14 years of age.'

Inspector Morgan also pointed out that there were instances of girls of only 11 and 12 years of age being approached in the streets by men offering them money. Having been thus introduced into such practices it was claimed that these girls then largely kept the company of the older girls, adopting their life-style.

A Superintendent at Whitechapel also stated that many of the younger girls followed their older friends and that there was little evidence of them being forced into such activities. He, like Henry Mayhew, pointed to the fact that many girls worked by day and resorted to prostitution on a casual or regular basis in their free time. Once again, there seemed to be ample evidence that the families involved were well aware of the girl's activities. 'Superior luxuries and dress', as it was described, played a large part in the spread of prostitution.

The Investigation into prostitution amongst the young took evidence from several sources working against this trade. In many cases it was pointed out that neither parents nor children involved recognised it as immoral. Instead, it was seen as a realistic way of earning money. The poor home background and the constant exposure of the young to cynical, and easy familiarity with those directly involved in prostitution, often made for an environment that accepted without question. The fact that the police were frequently powerless to prevent it was also a

Midnight scene, London's Haymarket during the middle years of the nineteenth century. The Haymarket was a favourite location for prostitutes to meet their clients, and was also well-known for its reputation as a location for child prostitution.

factor. Whilst it was an offence to blatantly solicit on the streets, most people who were offended by it were apparently reluctant to press charges for fear of loss of respectability.

The investigations into the problems of prostitution did devote some time to the question of girls being taken out of the country for purposes of immorality. Under the illusion that they were leaving England for marriage or for attractive employment many girls found themselves, instead, inmates of brothels in Belgium, Holland or France. Many did return as a result of efforts on their behalf as the evidence given to the House of Lords Committee shows. William Stead's notorious action of removing 13 year old Eliza Armstrong to the continent in order to demonstrate how easily it could be done is a well known example of the issue of the trade in girls. Whilst admonished by Josephine Butler, tireless campaigner for action on behalf of girls, Stead also received a prison sentence for his unusual efforts.

One area where useful progress was made was that of removing children from parents who kept brothels. Portsmouth has particular success in this respect. Here the Industrial Schools Amendment Act of 1880 was applied with determination. A committee of gentlemen purchased a freehold house with land at Waterloo, near Purbrook, seven miles from Portsmouth, and two ladies with experience of reformatory work offered their services without pay. These institutions aimed to give direction and guidance to all manner of abandoned or otherwise neglected children through a strict moral climate and a programme of useful vocational training to suit their circumstances.

In one well publicised case brought before the magistrates in 1882 five children were taken out of premises known to be used as a brothel. Their accommodation was described as a 'perfect den' being two rooms, one above the other, with one broken chair and an old table comprising the entire furniture. Despite the sordid surroundings

prostitution was carried on there, two prostitutes using the upstairs room divided off from the mother and her children by a thin partition whilst the other used the coal area downstairs. In response to questioning by the magistrate the mother stated that she maintained the children by the money gained from the prostitutes using the house.

The children were subsequently removed to the Industrial School with the exception of the eldest, a girl of about 12 years of age. Described as 'an idiot, and distorted in body, a hopeless cripple', this girl was eventually sent to an asylum.

Authorities in many other parts of the country were not necessarily as committed to the Act as those at Portsmouth. In evidence to the House of Lords Committee, Miss Ellice Hopkins, a vigilant campaigner on behalf of young girls, criticised the magistrates. In her view, the magistrates were frequently unwilling to commit children to Industrial Schools because of the expense involved. It was also her argument that many girls were being lost to prostitution because of apathy, indifference or direct open neglect. Despite the fact that the Industrial Schools Act was intended for the purpose of removing children from housing known to be used as a brothel, the evidence showed the reluctance of many magistrates to take the children from their parents.

The Criminal Law Amendment Act of 1885 succeeded in raising the age of consent to 16 years of age. Fifteen years earlier a Royal Commission had sought to raise the age from 12 to 14 to help counter the problem. For large numbers of young girls, however, the age of consent must have had little meaning or reference. As numerous interested individuals and groups pointed out, prostitution, as such, frequently developed out of the casual promiscuity and easy or enforced intimacy prevalent amongst certain sections of the working community both at home and at work.

Two street scenes showing life amongst the poor in London, 1875. Such circumstances often had a sense of despair or hopelessness amongst many when living in conditions of material and moral deprivation. Extremely close confinement, easy familiarity and significantly, economic hardship, could often create a real sense of community and identity, despite the difficulties. It could also, however, provide the means whereby children were subject to wanton exploitation, as in the widespread incidence of child prostitution common to the period.

Chapter Eleven
Crime and Punishment – Parkhurst Prison

'To witness the exertion of philanthropic enlightenment to reclaim juvenile offenders from ways of error to paths of virtue and peace is one of the most gratifying scenes of philanthropy to be enjoyed in this great Christian country.'

Such was the verdict of the *Illustrated London News* of March 1847 after inspecting and reporting on the system for young offenders at Parkhurst Prison on the Isle of Wight.

Parkhurst offered an excellent opportunity to study something of the Mid-Victorian response to young offenders and reflected the highly regulated regime in prisons of the period. The Prisons Reform Act of 1835 opened the way to considerations of the purpose, character and conduct of prison life which, in turn, led to the creation of the 'model' establishments of the period.

Pentonville, for example, was one such model, nationally, whilst at a more regional level, county prisons were adapted to enforce the 'separate' and 'silent' systems. Prisoners served their sentence in what was perpetual isolation as part of the overall plan to break down their criminal past and reshape their lives. Work, strict routine and constant supervision defined the prisoners' existence and to a certain extent this pattern of life, enforced upon adults, also applied to the young people at Parkhurst.

The prison was opened in 1838 and was sited on the Newport to West Cowes road, 1½ miles from Newport

itself. The original buildings had formed the hospital for a barracks close by, but major additions were commenced in 1843. These consisted of a chapel, probationary and junior wards, an infirmary and accommodation for the surgeon, assistant chaplain, steward and warders. The new buildings were of brick and cement dressings, whilst a wall 15 feet in height, enclosed the site. A figure of £30,000 was given for the new building which also included roads constructed to serve the complex.

New prisoners began their sentence in the Receiving Room with its slipper bath, fumigating apparatus and hot water. The prisoner was medically examined, washed and cleansed, then clothed in probationary dress.

Once admitted, the boys entered the Probationary Ward. This consisted of a large corridor of three tiers providing 137 cells. Each cell was 11 feet by 7 ft, and 8 ft 6 inches in height and contained the following items: A coconut fibre hammock which at night was fastened from wall to wall, 15 inches from the ground, (the hammock was held in place by wall cleats) a small table, writing desk, Bible, prayer and hymn books, school books, slate and pencil. Morning and evening cards with prayers and hymns with copies for writing were also provided, as was a candlestick and Palmers candle.

Prisoners in the probationary ward took all their meals in their cells, leaving them only for the following periods: 1½ hours for exercise, 2½ hours in school, half an hour

General view of Parkhurst Prison in the 1840s.

DRESSES OF THE OFFICERS AND PRISONERS.

SHOEMAKERS' DEPARTMENT.

PRISONER'S CELL.

Illustrations of life at Parkhurst Prison, Isle of Wight, opened for children/young people in 1838 and continuing in use for that purpose until 1863. With the development of the Youthful Offenders Act of 1854, the stress was increasingly placed upon institutions on borstal lines, offering corrective training and gainful employment. Neither system offered any easy option, conditions at Parkhurst being similar in many respects to the corrective environment of the new model prison – Pentonville etc., where silence and strict separation were uppermost. The first illustration shows the general view of Parkhurst with young offenders being supervised at their work in the fields. Elsewhere, the illustrations cover all the main aspects of life and conditions in the prison – uniform and appearance, cells, dining hall, workroom, corridors, general ward, probationary ward and chapel.

for cleaning and half an hour to attend chapel in the mornings. They were also strictly segregated in chapel. Whilst in their cells inmates were not permitted to be idle and were required to work at tailoring or shoemaking, for example, to ensure they used their time positively.

Outside each cell door was a card with prisoner's details displayed, ie. name, number, admission date and place of committal. Two dark cells were located in the basement for purposes of punishment and correction.

Prison uniform consisted of a leather cap with the inmate's number displayed in brass. Trousers and jacket were made of grey cloth with the letters P.P. sewn into the left breast and left thigh. A striped shirt, leather stock waistcoat for winter, worsted socks, and boots completed the uniform, all being supplied from within the prison.

Parkhurst considered its programme of employment to be very effective with the young people, the intention being to teach them a useful trade, vital to their rehabilitation. The workshops were said to be run with military precision. The following list, with the number of boys involved, illustrated the range of employment offered within the prison.

THE CHAPEL.

Brickmakers	20	Bricklayers	24
Bricklayers lab	24	Tailors	4
Shoemakers	60	including 208 juniors	
Cooks assistants	10	Bakers	16
Carpenters	32	Sawyers	12
Gardners	24	Painters	6
Blacksmiths	8	Agricultural lab	34

The inmates chosen for these duties were those considered to demonstrate the best conduct. All other prisoners were given what were termed 'lower prison duties', these being kitchen working and cleaning together with pumping. The latter was the pumping of water from the pump house in front of the main building. Twelve prisoners worked at the pumps changing on ten minute shifts. The water supplied the prison's needs and was yet another aspect of the overall programme aimed at achieving a high degree of self-sufficiency. Outside gangs, such as those in the fields, were given oakum picking duties during the wet weather – oakum being lengths of old rope which were cut into short pieces to be unpicked by the prisoners. The rope, known as 'junk', was weighed before being distributed to ensure uniform measure to each prisoner.

For 2½ hours on alternate days the boys received religious and moral instruction in the school room. Apart from eight open desks where they could see and be seen freely, the boys were sat in some 50 compartments, shut off from one another, effectively isolating them from all but the teacher. Those who showed interest and good behaviour generally could graduate to the General Ward school. Here tuition was given for 5 hours on alternate days, but on one day a week all instruction was given in the cells with the afternoon period being given over to knitting and practical pursuits.

In the school itself the inmates were taught the principles of Scripture biography, Sacred geography, Scripture history, emblems, parables, arithmetic, writing and general knowledge, etymology grammar and music. Lessons were both written and oral. A library was attached to the school, and was mainly used on Sundays for reading and study.

THE CORRIDOR.

The Middlesex Industrial School, Feltham, 1866. Following the Industrial Schools Act of 1854, certain counties took active steps to implement measures. Middlesex was one; 33 resident, and 13 non-resident officers were responsible for some 560 boys. The scene here is that of the annual inspection by the county magistrate.

As with all the modern prisons of the mid-century there was an emphasis upon a high standard of physical care, which often went far beyond that experienced on the outside. The cells were warm and clean. Likewise, the boys enjoyed meals often superior to anything that many could expect at home. Soup, bread, potatoes, rice, cooked meat and cocoa were items that would have been welcome on many an agricultural labourer's table, for example. A mudlark on the Thames, in conversation with Henry Mayhew, expressed his preference for prison life over that of the river during winter. To be fed, clothed, educated and sheltered in prison had obvious advantages and serves to give some perspective when looking back at the period from our own time.

Whilst prison life for young people was not, nor was ever intended to be, an easy option, the strict discipline and highly institutionalised environment must be measured against the standards and experience of the day. Parkhurst was not used for juvenile offenders from 1863, onwards. With the introduction of the Reformatories Act of 1866 a new dimension or direction was apparent. The Rev. Sidney Turner, as Inspector to the new reformatory institutions described their purpose, the inmates being those between 10 and 16 years of age:

'They are institutions for the custody, corrective training and industrial instruction of their inmates; in fact, a species of juvenile houses of correction. The intellectual teaching which forms the staple of ordinary schools is a very small element in their constitution. The task which the managers of reformatories undertake is chiefly the exercise of such moral and industrial discipline after the discharge of the inmates as will ensure them a fair start in some honest line of livelihood.'

The apparent paradox of some young people actually preferring life, or many aspects of life within prison, is largely explained by reference to working and living conditions outside. With the obvious exception that prisoners were deprived of their liberty, their physical circumstances could often be superior to certain forms of employment within industry and agriculture.

The additional irony is that despite the deterrent theory behind penal institutions, (and indeed, the workhouse) – that of making life as unattractive as possible, it did often represent an improvement for many inmates. At Parkhurst, the sense of discipline and purpose, supported by the policy of useful work and training, could serve to give young offenders meaningful objectives. Through a host of random circumstances – poverty, environment, illness etc., many young people in the outside world were prevented from realising any ambitions or potential and despite the strict limitation on freedom of movement, prison life could sometimes work to their advantage. To conclude, it would be interesting to discover just how far contemporary society appreciated these ironies and what conclusion they drew from them.

APPENDIX

Rules of the Walkden Moor Servants' School, near Worsley, Lancashire.

GENERAL RULES.

1. The girls must be down stairs half an hour after they are called in the morning, each girl having said a private prayer, turned down her bed, and opened the window, before leaving her chamber. They will wash themselves in their rooms, and go to their work till the time of family prayer. Half an hour is allowed for breakfast, then work till twelve. Dinner at one o'clock. An hour is allowed for dinner and recreation till two o'clock, when work commences, to continue until half-past four in winter and five in summer. When school is over, the school-room is to be swept. The girls work or knit till supper-time. After supper needle-work, writing, and ciphering, till family prayer, they will then go to bed; and after their private prayers, no conversation is allowed.

2. On Sunday, after leaving their room, each girl will be expected to look out the psalms and lessons for the day, and read over lessons prepared for school, before going to breakfast, and at nine o'clock they go to the Sunday-school. They dine between the services, and if there be any time before going to afternoon school, each girl will be expected to find out the text of the morning's sermon in her Bible. Afterwards, to have a tract read aloud to them, and go to bed at eight in winter. In summer, to take a walk after supper. No girl will be permitted to leave the house unaccompanied by the matron or parent.

3. See Diet Table.

WORKING DEPARTMENT.

4. One girl kitchen-maid, one fortnight; one girl, housemaid a fortnight; two girls, laundry-maids a fortnight. At the end of the fortnight each girl changes her department. A girl from the school takes the place of the kitchen-maid—the kitchen-maid of the last fortnight becomes housemaid—the housemaids become laundry-maids, and those who were laundry-maids go into the school.

5. The kitchen-maid to go at once to the kitchen after she is dressed in the morning, with her working-apron. She is to lay down her hearth-cloth, clean the irons, and rub over the stove, light the fire, fill the boiler, set on the kettle; then sweep the kitchen, and scour away carefully any dirty spot. After breakfast, make the preparations for baking, dinner, &c.

6. The elder housemaid, as soon as dressed, is to sweep the school-room, dust, and air it; which is also to be scoured every Wednesday and Saturday after school-hours, when the housemaid will be assisted by all the boarders.

The younger housemaid is to assist in sweeping the school-room. They both occupy themselves in the parlour, rubbing the furniture, and dusting the room; she then prepares the breakfast-table. After breakfast both girls go to the bed-rooms. The beds are to be made up well, but briskly, not talking over their work. The younger housemaid is to go into school immediately the beds are made. Every Friday the grates are to be polished, and the bed-rooms scoured. Except on Fridays, all the household work must be done by eleven o'clock, and both housemaids are to be in the school.

7. The laundry-maids must rise an hour earlier on Tuesday morning to wash. On Wednesday they will dry what they can of the clothes the same afternoon, fold, and prepare for ironing. On Thursday they must iron, and by Thursday night all the ironing must be finished. The elder girl is to sort the linen, and place each portion on the proper shelf. They fill their copper on Monday night. The laundry-maids are to darn the table-linen, towels, stockings, &c.; the ironing-cloth and irons are under their charge. The first laundry-maid is to have, during the fortnight she is in office, the superintendence of the clothes-presses, and is to be accountable for their order, and for the correctness of the number of the clothes.

8. Saturday.—After breakfast, when the usual morning work is over, the school-room is to be scoured. The girls then work in the garden till twelve. At twelve read the psalms for the following day. After dinner, work in the garden. Single lesson from four till half-past five. Work until supper time. After supper, wash their feet and go to bed.

RULES FOR THE SCHOOL-GIRLS.

Rise at half-past five in the summer, and six in the winter; half-an-hour allowed for washing, dressing, and private prayer.

Until breakfast-bell rings, look over lessons, or work in the garden.

From breakfast till nine o'clock, recreation.

Nine o'clock till half-past twelve, school. After school, work in the garden till the dinner-bell rings, and after dinner recreation till two.

Two o'clock till five, afternoon school.

At five o'clock, knit till supper-time. After supper, cipher, write, learn lessons, work (mending, &c.) till bed-time.

On Wednesdays and Saturdays singing lessons.

On Saturdays, girls to assist the working girls to scour the school-room.

Rules for the Matron.

1. The girls are all to be treated with strict impartiality, and great care must be taken to suppress any indication of envy or jealousy apparent in any of their dispositions.

2. The girls are to change their working department every Friday fortnight, when the rules of the institution are to be publicly read through by the matron, who is also to see that each girl delivers up her trust in good order to her successor.

3. The matron must keep herself in constant active service the whole morning, attending to the different departments of service, and to each alike, keeping each girl strictly to her own time of service, however dull or incapable she may at first appear to be.

4. Never to permit a girl to be idle for a moment, except during the hours of recreation. The girls must not be allowed to stand over the fire. The matron must be careful that they use the privilege of air and exercise at the permitted hours.

5. The matron must carefully note down any misdemeanour or breach of rules that she may observe in any of the girls in the course of the day ; also the smallest approach to deception or untruth. She must also note down when the servants are behind in their work.

6. The matron must see that the servants come into school clean from their work, and punctually to their time.

7. The matron is never to allow any of the girls to leave the school to visit their friends, or under any pretence whatever, except by order of the clergyman; neither is she allowed to send them on errands to the shop, or elsewhere.

8. The matron is to see that every Tuesday each girl has her brush and comb clean, having been washed in the soapsuds that morning ; also, every Saturday, all the girls are to thoroughly clean their heads, and at night the laundry-maid is to fill the boiler and pour the hot water into the tubs for all the girls to wash their feet before going to bed.

9. The matron is never to omit going round to see that every girl is in bed by a quarter to nine, when she takes away the light.

10. The matron must be careful that they do not exceed the time allowed for meals.

Times for Ringing the Bell.

Half-past five in summer, six in winter, for the servants to get up.
Half an hour afterwards to ring for the school-girls to get up.
Quarter before eight for washing hands.
Ten minutes before eight for prayers,
Nine'oclock for school.
Five minutes before one for washing hands and smoothing hair.
One o'clock dinner in summer, quarter before one in winter.

Two o'clock for afternoon school.
Half-past six for supper.
Quarter past eight for prayers.

Arrangement of Time for the Servants.

Rise at half-past five in summer, and six in winter ; half an hour allowed for dressing, &c. Work commences at six in summer, and half-past six in winter.

Before breakfast, the kitchen-maid is to lay down her hearth-rug, clean the irons, rub the stove, light the fire, set on the kettle, sweep the kitchen, scour away the spots, clean the knives and forks in the back kitchen, and clean the candlesticks.

The housemaids sweep the school-room, dust and air it, light the fire, sweep the parlour, rub the furniture, dust the room, and clean the clogs, and prepare the breakfast-table.

The laundry-maids, on Monday morning, clean the Sunday shoes ; on other mornings they will be engaged washing, folding, or ironing, as may be required.

Quarter before eight o'clock bell.—Every girl leaves her work, washes her hands, and goes into the school-room for family prayer.

Eight till half-past eight.—Breakfast.

Half-past eight till half-past twelve.—The kitchen-maid is to clean the front steps, scour the passage, and make preparations for baking, dinner, &c.

The housemaids are to clear away and wash up the breakfast things, go to the bed-rooms, make the beds, sweep the rooms, empty the basins, and refill them for the washing on the following morning, and be ready to go into school by eleven, except on Friday, when the grates are to be polished, and the rooms scoured.

The laundry-maids, every Monday, the first thing after breakfast, are to look up the linen, count it over, and carefully examine if anything require mending, that it may be done that day in readiness for the wash on Tuesday. On Friday they will be in school during all the school-hours.

Half-past twelve till one.—The kitchen-maid is to wash her hands, and prepare for serving dinner.

The housemaids are to get the knives and forks, plates, dishes, and all that will be required for dinner, and at a quarter before one, lay the cloth.

The laundry-maids are to continue at their business until the bell rings.

Five minutes to one.—Every girl is to wash her hands, and make herself neat for dinner.

One o'clock, dinner, and by two o'clock the things must be cleared away. The housemaids to clear the table, and carry the things to the kitchen-maid, who washes up, having first put all all the eatables in the larder. The kitchen-maid then sweeps the kitchen, makes up the fire, puts on the kettle, cleans herself, and must be in school by three o'clock.

DIET TABLE.

Breakfast—Sunday, Monday, Wednesday, and Friday, one pint of cocoa, half-a-pound of bread, or ten ounces to the elder girls. Tuesday, Thursday, and Saturday, oatmeal porridge, one pound of bread, half-a-pint of milk.

Dinner.—Monday: Half-a-pint of meat, two pounds of potatoes, six ounces of bread.

Tuesday: Suet pudding, and greens from the gardens.

Wednesday: Pea-soup.

Thursday: Same as Monday.

Friday: Rice pudding.

Saturday: Pea-soup.

Sunday: Potato-pie, baked on Saturday.

Supper.—Eight ounces of bread, ten ounces for the elder girls, one ounce and a half of cheese, and water, three evenings; the other three evenings they have bread and treacle, or dripping, and half-a-pint of milk; on Sunday they have for supper tea and carraway bread, or bread and dripping.

ARTICLES OF CLOTHING.—Three shifts, 3 night ditto, 3 night caps, 2 under petticoats, 1 linsey petticoat, 5 jackets, 4 pocket handkerchiefs, 4 check aprons, 1 white one, 3 pairs grey stockings, 1 pair clogs, 1 pair in-door shoes, 1 pair Sunday shoes, 4 working aprons, 2 pairs stays, 1 bonnet, 1 bonnet cap, 1 cloak, 1 working petticoat, 4 neckerchiefs.

PENALTIES.—For swearing at, or calling the matron names, for dishonesty, deceitful conduct, or resistance to authority, to be suspended from her next turn as servant, and not allowed to see her friends the following visiting day. Upon a second offence of the same nature, the matron is to report it to the minister: and upon the third, the girl is to be expelled.

The following is to be read by such girls as are about to enter the school, and to their parents :—

Address to the Girls on their admission to Walkden Moor Servants' School.

On entering this school to learn the office of servants, you have promised to endeavour to observe the following rules with the greatest strictness and attention :—

1. You must obey your matron in everything, not answering again.

   " Exhort servants to be obedient unto their masters, and to please them well in all things : not answering again."—TITUS ii. 9.

2. You must speak the truth.

   " Wherefore putting away lying, speak every man truth with his neighbour : for ye are members one of another."—EPHESIANS iv. 25.

3. You must be honest, keeping your hands from picking and stealing.

   " Recompense to no man evil for evil. Provide things honest in the sight of all men." ROMANS xii. 18.

Also the Eighth Commandment :—

   " Thou shalt not steal."

4. You must govern your tongues, keeping your mouths from evil-speaking, lying, and slandering.

   " But above all things, my brethren, swear not ; neither by heaven, neither by the earth, neither by any other oath : but let your yea be yea, and your nay be nay ; lest ye fall into condemnation."—JAMES v. 12.

Aso the Third Commandment :—

   " Thou shalt not take the name of the LORD thy GOD in vain."

5. You must speak civilly and kindly one to another.

   " A soft answer turneth away wrath : but grievous words stir up anger."—PROVERBS xv. 1.

6. You must bear being told of your faults.

   " Poverty and shame shall be to him that refuseth instruction ; but he that regardeth reproof shall be honoured."—PROVERBS xiii. 18.

7. You must avoid idleness.

   " Not slothful in business ; fervent in spirit ; serving the LORD."—ROMANS xii. 2.
   " Slothfulness casteth into a deep sleep ; and an idle soul shall suffer hunger."—PROVERBS xix.

8. You are not allowed to leave the house without asking **leave of the matron**.

If any of you break these rules, the matron will note your name and offence in her book; and, according to the character in her book, you will be first or last to be recommended t~ situations in service when they offer.

ADVICE TO THE PARENTS.

When your children are admitted to the WALKDEN MOOR SERVANTS' SCHOOL, it is expected of you that you should assist your children in keeping the rules which they have agreed to before entering the school; and this you may do by attending to the following advice:—

How to assist in Rule 1.—Be careful yourself to speak respectfully to the matron; never allow your child to bring home idle tales, or to speak evil of her when she is not present to say whether it be true or not. Remember the Scripture:—

> "Thou shalt not go up and down as a tale-bearer among thy people; neither shalt thou stand against the blood of thy neighbour: I am the LORD."—LEVIT. xix. 16.
>
> "The north wind driveth away rain; so doth an angry countenance a backbiting tongue."—PROVERBS xxv. 23.

How to assist in Rule 2.—Be very careful that your child never speaks an untruth at home. Remember:—

> "Lying lips are an abomination to the LORD: but they that deal truly are His delight."—PROVERBS xii. 22.

How to assist in Rule 3.—Be very careful that your child never brings home anything that does not belong to her. If you have reason to think that she has come by anything unfairly, search out the matter, and restore the thing to its proper owner.

> "Whoso is partner with a thief, hateth his own soul."—PROVERBS xxix. 24.
>
> "Though hand join in hand, the wicked shall not go unpunished."—PROVERBS xi. 21.

How to assist in Rule 4.—Be very careful that your child never hears you giving way to angry words and evil speaking. Remember:—

> "He that is slow to wrath is of great understanding; but he that is hasty of spirit exalteth folly."—PROVERBS xiv. 29.
>
> "He that hath no rule over his own spirit is like a city that is broken down, and without walls."—PROVERBS xxv. 28.

How to assist in Rule 5.—Never allow your child to bring home unkind and ill-natured stories of her fellow-servants or school-fellows. Remember:—

> "In many things we offend all."—JAMES iii. 2.

Therefore see that she acts upon our LORD's rule:—

> "Therefore all things whatsoever ye would that men should do unto you, do ye even so to them."—MATTHEW vii. 12.

How to assist in Rule 6.—Believe that your child has the faults she has been corrected for, though you may not have observed them, and be willing to have her corrected for them. Remember:—

> "The rod and reproof give wisdom; but a child left to himself bringeth his mother to shame."—PROVERBS xxix. 15.

How to assist in Rule 7.—You may tell whether your children are idle by their complaining of work. Remember:—

> "The way of the slothful man is an hedge of thorns."—PROVERBS xv. 19.
>
> "The slothful man saith, There is a lion without, I shall be slain in the streets."—PROVERBS

Which means that the idle and slothful see hardships and difficulties in everything. Remember:—

> "For even when we were with you, this we commanded you, that if any would not work, neither should he eat."—2 THESSALONIANS iii. 10.

How to assist in Rule 8.—Never go yourself, nor allow any of your family to go to the school, except on the days allowed; and never permit your child to come home, except on the days she has leave. If she comes home without leave, send her back instantly.

You are requested to read over this paper on the morning that you go to the school, or when your child is coming home.

No male relation but the father will be permitted to visit the girls.

After going to see their friends with leave, they must return by eight o'clock precisely. It is requested that the father or mother will see their daughter home.

———

Acknowledgements

Many people have helped in the preparation of this book. Terry Knight, Joanne and Kim at the Cornish Studies Library, Redruth, have, as always, been extremely helpful, organising inter-library loans to make my work considerably easier than it might have been. Special thanks also go to the Penzance Subscription Library, Morrab Gardens and to Lesley Lowden and Annabelle Read for their interest and co-operation throughout. This library has been of immense help to me, being one of the best research centres in the west of England, superbly resourced and staffed. Unlimited access to *The Illustrated London News* and to *Punch*, together with the detailed findings of Royal Commissions and other nineteenth century literary works has been vital to the overall content and style of this book. The magnificent *Illustrated London News* and *Punch* should be essential reading for anyone considering study of Victorian social and economic history.

My mother-in-law, Kathleen Ingram, and my brother and sister-in-law, Rob and Angela, have also made important contributions through their research on my behalf in Norwich and Manchester. Margaret Barron must be thanked for typing the entire manuscript and for coping with numerous additions and alterations along the way; thanks also to Peter White for the cover design, and to David George of Radio Cornwall for his continued interest in the project. I must also acknowledge Roy Davies and Derek Towers of BBC2 'Timewatch' for taking up the project whilst it was still in preparation and thereby giving tremendous encouragement by adapting it for television. I would also thank Roger Hardingham for the opportunity to get the work published, and for his interest throughout.

Finally, I would thank my wife, Jo, for encouraging me throughout this work, for reading and discussing numerous ideas and approaches and helping me clarify my thoughts on the material generally. The original idea for the book was hers.

Alan Bennett
June 1991

Distribution of tea, coffee, bread and cheese to the poor, late at night in London's Trafalgar Square, October 1887. An orderly gathering of between four and five hundred people, men, women and children, were provided for on the east side of the square. "It was evident", said the *Illustrated London News* "from the manner in which most of the poor people devoured their portions, that they were in a condition little short of starvation." The provisions were paid for by costermongers who had collected the sum of three pounds to buy the goods.